M000315417

Christmas Bible Readings

Christmas Bible Readings
Scriptures Curated for Daily Advent Reflection

Norma Jesus

Cruz Media
2013

Copyright © 2013 by Norma Jesus

All rights reserved. This book or any portion thereof may not be repro-
duced or used in any manner whatsoever without the express written
permission of the publisher except for the use of brief quotations in a
book review or scholarly journal.

Scripture quotations are from the *ESV® Bible (The Holy Bible, English
Standard Version®)*, copyright© 2001 by Crossway Bibles, a publishing
ministry of Good News Publishers. Used by permission. All rights reserved.

Cover photo provided by Christ Church, Plano, TX. Used with permission
(Rev. Canon David H. Roseberry).

First Printing: 2013

ISBN 978-0-615-91541-8

Cruz Media
Plano, TX

www.christmasbiblereadings.com

Dedication

For my children, John, Noah, and Elias:
May you always love and live in the Word.

With gratitude and love to
my husband John and my sister Sandy.
Without your encouragement and help I would
never have finished this project.

Contents

Acknowledgements

This book was made possible by the generous patronage of many supporters, including those listed below.

Timothy Phan
Karl Slaman
Anonymous #1
Pat Ross
W.B. Allen, Ph.D
Sandy Vargas
Lucas and Cherie Morel
Cousins Cathy and Elizabeth
Marc and Wendy Boas
 (2Cor9:8-10)

City Church, Joshua, TX
Cecelia
'Cross'
Spencer Anthony
Sharon Beeman
Letitia Boas
John and Elizabeth Eastman
Aili Gardea
Mark Hagood
Sandy Hotz
Gregory T. Huffman
J.J. Jesus
Stephen Mubita
Tuan Nguyen
Juan Romeo Riojas
Jennifer Scott

Special thanks to Crossway Bibles for granting permission for the extensive use of the *ESV*® *Bible* throughout this book. Bible verse references for each daily reading are provided to encourage readers to study the complete text from their personal Bibles.

What is Advent and How to Use This Book

The Advent Season

Advent, the Latin word for *coming* or *arrival*, has been celebrated for centuries in many Christian churches as a time of spiritual preparation for Christmas. The focus of the season is on Scriptures that foretold Jesus' birth and anticipate His return. The traditional elements of Advent are Scripture reading, prayer, song, and a wreath with five candles.

The Advent season begins the fourth Sunday before Christmas and culminates on Christmas Day. During Advent, many churches display a special arrangement of candles and during each of the Sunday church services of the season, one or more candles are ceremoniously lit while reading Scripture or singing a Christmas hymn.

The Advent season is also an excellent time at home for individuals or families to focus on Christ's birth and return. This book is meant to facilitate that effort with a collection of readings that will take the reader from Bible passages in the Book of Genesis, (*the beginning*) to promises of a Messiah from the lineage of David through the birth of Jesus and prophecies of His return and our time with Him eternally. Each reading is designed so that it can be read in one sitting, and suggestions for prayer, song, and discussion are included.

Advent has been celebrated in varied ways and traditions over the centuries. A wreath and candles are nice, but not necessary. This book offers merely one way to celebrate. The point is to attempt to spend time focusing on God each day.

Advent Candles

Advent candles are usually arranged in a circle as part of an evergreen wreath with the colored candles on the outside and the white candle in the middle. The wreath can be displayed in a prominent place where an individual or family will see it often and easily gather around it for the daily readings. The shortening of the candles is a great visual for the shortening of time until Christmas and the celebration of the arrival of Christ. The circular shape and the evergreens are reminders of God's eternal existence and the promise that believers will have everlasting life with Him. Although a wreath of evergreens is traditional, there are many other beautiful wreaths available and many families make their own. The color of candles used and the order in which the colors are used varies. What each candle or week of celebration is called also varies.

Organization of This Book

This book is organized with a theme for each week.
· Fourth Sunday before Christmas: The Grace Candle (Purple)
· Third Sunday before Christmas: The Joy Candle (Purple)
· Second Sunday before Christmas: The Hope Candle (Pink)
· First Sunday before Christmas: The Peace Candle (Purple)
· Christmas (or Christmas Eve): The Love Candle (White)

On the fourth Sunday before Christmas, the first purple candle will be lighted and will remain lit while reading the scripture for that day. This same candle will be relit each day for the daily readings.

The third Sunday before Christmas, the first candle and the second purple candle will be lighted and will be lit for the readings of that week.

The second Sunday before Christmas, the first two purple candles and the pink candle will be lighted and remain lit for the readings of that week.

The first Sunday before Christmas, the first three candles and the last purple candle will be lighted and remain lit for the readings of that week.

On Christmas Day, the white candle or the white candle and all the colored candles will be lit and remain lit for the readings and prayers, and for as long as you wish that day.

Suggestion for families or groups

- Take turns lighting and extinguishing the candles.
- Have each member take part in the reading.
- Take turns leading the prayer or have each person share in praying aloud.
- Have each person pray for someone outside the family each day or week.
- Act out scenes from the readings.
- Discuss the meaning of the song for the week. Substitute your own choice of song if there is one that is more meaningful to you or your family.
- Make the Advent Season a time of doing for others:
  - Provide a service for someone in need; it could be a more formal act, such as volunteering through a charitable organization, or as simple as writing a card of encouragement to someone.
  - Donate to a charity. Each person could sacrifice something they would normally spend money on for themselves and send that to a charity instead.

Grace

Light the first purple candle

And the Word became flesh and dwelt among us, and we have seen his glory, glory as of the only Son from the Father, full of grace and truth.

John 1:14

We may think of the Old Testament as the Bible record of events before Jesus and the New Testament as recording events from Jesus' birth on, but Scripture tells us of His presence from the beginning. From the first man there was sin, but by God's grace there was also, from the beginning, the promise of reconciliation through the Christ.

Suggestions for the week

- Sing *O Come, O Come, Emmanuel.*
- Meditate on the power of the written and spoken word.
- Be mindful of how the words you speak affect others.
- Purpose to use your words in a positive way this week: to encourage, to instruct, to share God's love and truth.

Pray that God will reveal His truth to you as you read the Scriptures.

Read: Genesis1:1-2:3; John 1:1-5; Ephesians 2:10

^{1} In the beginning, God created the heavens and the earth. ^{2} The earth was without form and void, and darkness was over the face of the deep. And the Spirit of God was hovering over the face of the waters.

^{3} And God said, "Let there be light," and there was light. ^{4} And God saw that the light was good. And God separated the light from the darkness. ^{5} God called the light Day, and the darkness he called Night. And there was evening and there was morning, the first day.

^{6} And God said, "Let there be an expanse in the midst of the waters, and let it separate the waters from the waters." ^{7} And God made the expanse and separated the waters that were under the expanse from the waters that were above the expanse. And it was so. ^{8} And God called the expanse Heaven. And there was evening and there was morning, the second day.

^{9} And God said, "Let the waters under the heavens be gathered together into one place, and let the dry land appear." And it was so. ^{10} God called the dry land Earth, and the waters that were gathered together he called Seas. And God saw that it was good.

^{11} And God said, "Let the earth sprout vegetation, plants yielding seed, and fruit trees bearing fruit in which is their seed, each according to its kind, on the earth." And it was so. ^{12} The earth brought forth vegetation, plants yielding seed according to their own kinds, and trees bearing fruit in which is their seed, each according to its kind. And God saw that it was good. *13* And there was evening and there was morning, the third day.

14 And God said, "Let there be lights in the expanse of the heavens to separate the day from the night. And let them be for signs and for seasons, and for days and years, *15* and let them be lights in the expanse of the heavens to give light upon the earth." And it was so. *16* And God made the two great lights—the greater light to rule the day and the lesser light to rule the night—and the stars. *17* And God set them in the expanse of the heavens to give light on the earth, *18* to rule over the day and over the night, and to separate the light from the darkness. And God saw that it was good. *19* And there was evening and there was morning, the fourth day.

20 And God said, "Let the waters swarm with swarms of living creatures, and let birds fly above the earth across the expanse of the heavens." *21* So God created the great sea creatures and every living creature that moves, with which the waters swarm, according to their kinds, and every winged bird according to its kind. And God saw that it was good. *22* And God blessed them, saying, "Be fruitful and multiply and fill the waters in the seas, and let birds multiply on the earth." *23* And there was evening and there was morning, the fifth day.

24 And God said, "Let the earth bring forth living creatures according to their kinds—livestock and creeping things and beasts of the earth according to their kinds." And it was so. *25* And God made the beasts of the earth according to their kinds and the livestock according to their kinds, and everything that creeps on the ground according to its kind. And God saw that it was good.

²⁶ Then God said, "Let us make man in our image, after our likeness. And let them have dominion over the fish of the sea and over the birds of the heavens and over the livestock and over all the earth and over every creeping thing that creeps on the earth."

²⁷ So God created man in his own image, in the image of God he created him; male and female he created them.

²⁸ And God blessed them. And God said to them, "Be fruitful and multiply and fill the earth and subdue it, and have dominion over the fish of the sea and over the birds of the heavens and over every living thing that moves on the earth." ²⁹ And God said, "Behold, I have given you every plant yielding seed that is on the face of all the earth, and every tree with seed in its fruit. You shall have them for food. ³⁰ And to every beast of the earth and to every bird of the heavens and to everything that creeps on the earth, everything that has the breath of life, I have given every green plant for food." And it was so. ³¹ And God saw everything that he had made, and behold, it was very good. And there was evening and there was morning, the sixth day.

¹ Thus the heavens and the earth were finished, and all the host of them. ² And on the seventh day God finished his work that he had done, and he rested on the seventh day from all his work that he had done. ³ So God blessed the seventh day and made it holy, because on it God rested from all his work that he had done in creation.

John

¹ In the beginning was the Word, and the Word was with God, and the Word was God. ² He was in the beginning with God. ³ All things were made through him, and without him was not any thing made that was made. ⁴ In him was life, and the life was the

light of men. *5* The light shines in the darkness, and the darkness has not overcome it.

Ephesians

10 For we are his workmanship, created in Christ Jesus for good works, which God prepared beforehand, that we should walk in them.

Discuss: What do these verses teach you about God? What do these verses teach you about your relationship to God?

Pray that God will reveal His truth to you as you read the Scriptures.

Read: Genesis 2:7-9,21-3:24; Romans 5:15-19

⁷ Then the Lord God formed the man of dust from the ground and breathed into his nostrils the breath of life, and the man became a living creature. ⁸ And the Lord God planted a garden in Eden, in the east, and there he put the man whom he had formed. ⁹ And out of the ground the Lord God made to spring up every tree that is pleasant to the sight and good for food. The tree of life was in the midst of the garden, and the tree of the knowledge of good and evil.

²¹ So the Lord God caused a deep sleep to fall upon the man, and while he slept took one of his ribs and closed up its place with flesh. ²² And the rib that the Lord God had taken from the man he made into a woman and brought her to the man. ²³ Then the man said, "This at last is bone of my bones and flesh of my flesh; she shall be called Woman, because she was taken out of Man."

²⁴ Therefore a man shall leave his father and his mother and hold fast to his wife, and they shall become one flesh. ²⁵ And the man and his wife were both naked and were not ashamed.

¹ Now the serpent was more crafty than any other beast of the field that the Lord God had made.

He said to the woman, "Did God actually say, 'You shall not eat of any tree in the garden'?" ² And the woman said to the serpent, "We may eat of the fruit of the trees in the garden, ³ but

God said, 'You shall not eat of the fruit of the tree that is in the midst of the garden, neither shall you touch it, lest you die.'" *4* But the serpent said to the woman, "You will not surely die. *5* For God knows that when you eat of it your eyes will be opened, and you will be like God, knowing good and evil." *6* So when the woman saw that the tree was good for food, and that it was a delight to the eyes, and that the tree was to be desired to make one wise, she took of its fruit and ate, and she also gave some to her husband who was with her, and he ate. *7* Then the eyes of both were opened, and they knew that they were naked. And they sewed fig leaves together and made themselves loincloths.

8 And they heard the sound of the Lord God walking in the garden in the cool of the day, and the man and his wife hid themselves from the presence of the Lord God among the trees of the garden. *9* But the Lord God called to the man and said to him, "Where are you?" *10* And he said, "I heard the sound of you in the garden, and I was afraid, because I was naked, and I hid myself." *11* He said, "Who told you that you were naked? Have you eaten of the tree of which I commanded you not to eat?" *12* The man said, "The woman whom you gave to be with me, she gave me fruit of the tree, and I ate." *13* Then the Lord God said to the woman, "What is this that you have done?" The woman said, "The serpent deceived me, and I ate."

14 The Lord God said to the serpent,

"Because you have done this, cursed are you above all livestock and above all beasts of the field; on your belly you shall go, and dust you shall eat all the days of your life.

¹⁵ I will put enmity between you and the woman, and between your offspring and her offspring; he shall bruise your head, and you shall bruise his heel."

¹⁶ To the woman he said,

"I will surely multiply your pain in childbearing; in pain you shall bring forth children. Your desire shall be for your husband, and he shall rule over you."

¹⁷ And to Adam he said,

"Because you have listened to the voice of your wife and have eaten of the tree of which I commanded you, 'You shall not eat of it,' cursed is the ground because of you; in pain you shall eat of it all the days of your life;

¹⁸ thorns and thistles it shall bring forth for you; and you shall eat the plants of the field.

¹⁹ By the sweat of your face you shall eat bread, till you return to the ground, for out of it you were taken; for you are dust, and to dust you shall return."

²⁰ The man called his wife's name Eve, because she was the mother of all living. ²¹ And the Lord God made for Adam and for his wife garments of skins and clothed them.

²² Then the Lord God said, "Behold, the man has become like one of us in knowing good and evil. Now, lest he reach out his hand and take also of the tree of life and eat, and live forever—" ²³ therefore the Lord God sent him out from the garden of Eden to work the ground from which he was taken. ²⁴ He drove out the man, and at the east of the garden of Eden he placed the cheru-

bim and a flaming sword that turned every way to guard the way to the tree of life.

Romans

[15] But the free gift is not like the trespass. For if many died through one man's trespass, much more have the grace of God and the free gift by the grace of that one man Jesus Christ abounded for many. [16] And the free gift is not like the result of that one man's sin. For the judgment following one trespass brought condemnation, but the free gift following many trespasses brought justification. [17] For if, because of one man's trespass, death reigned through that one man, much more will those who receive the abundance of grace and the free gift of righteousness reign in life through the one man Jesus Christ.

[18] Therefore, as one trespass led to condemnation for all men, so one act of righteousness leads to justification and life for all men. [19] For as by the one man's disobedience the many were made sinners, so by the one man's obedience the many will be made righteous.

Discuss: What do these verses teach you about God? What do these verses teach you about your relationship to God?

Pray that God will reveal His truth to you as you read the Scriptures.

Read: Genesis 6:9-18; 7:1-5,11-24; 8:1-5,13-22; 9:1,8-13

⁹ These are the generations of Noah. Noah was a righteous man, blameless in his generation. Noah walked with God. ¹⁰ And Noah had three sons, Shem, Ham, and Japheth.

¹¹ Now the earth was corrupt in God's sight, and the earth was filled with violence. ¹² And God saw the earth, and behold, it was corrupt, for all flesh had corrupted their way on the earth. ¹³ And God said to Noah, "I have determined to make an end of all flesh, for the earth is filled with violence through them. Behold, I will destroy them with the earth. ¹⁴ Make yourself an ark of gopher wood. Make rooms in the ark, and cover it inside and out with pitch. ¹⁵ This is how you are to make it: the length of the ark 300 cubits, its breadth 50 cubits, and its height 30 cubits. ¹⁶ Make a roof for the ark, and finish it to a cubit above, and set the door of the ark in its side. Make it with lower, second, and third decks. ¹⁷ For behold, I will bring a flood of waters upon the earth to destroy all flesh in which is the breath of life under heaven. Everything that is on the earth shall die. ¹⁸ But I will establish my covenant with you, and you shall come into the ark, you, your sons, your wife, and your sons' wives with you.

¹ Then the Lord said to Noah, "Go into the ark, you and all your household, for I have seen that you are righteous before me in this generation. ² Take with you seven pairs of all clean animals, the male and his mate, and a pair of the animals that are

not clean, the male and his mate, *3* and seven pairs of the birds of the heavens also, male and female, to keep their offspring alive on the face of all the earth. *4* For in seven days I will send rain on the earth forty days and forty nights, and every living thing that I have made I will blot out from the face of the ground." *5* And Noah did all that the Lord had commanded him.

11 In the six hundredth year of Noah's life, in the second month, on the seventeenth day of the month, on that day all the fountains of the great deep burst forth, and the windows of the heavens were opened. *12* And rain fell upon the earth forty days and forty nights. *13* On the very same day Noah and his sons, Shem and Ham and Japheth, and Noah's wife and the three wives of his sons with them entered the ark, *14* they and every beast, according to its kind, and all the livestock according to their kinds, and every creeping thing that creeps on the earth, according to its kind, and every bird, according to its kind, every winged creature. *15* They went into the ark with Noah, two and two of all flesh in which there was the breath of life. *16* And those that entered, male and female of all flesh, went in as God had commanded him. And the Lord shut him in.

17 The flood continued forty days on the earth. The waters increased and bore up the ark, and it rose high above the earth. *18* The waters prevailed and increased greatly on the earth, and the ark floated on the face of the waters. *19* And the waters prevailed so mightily on the earth that all the high mountains under the whole heaven were covered. *20* The waters prevailed above the mountains, covering them fifteen cubits deep. *21* And all flesh died that moved on the earth, birds, livestock, beasts, all swarming creatures that swarm on the earth, and all mankind. *22* Everything on the dry land in whose nostrils was the breath of life died. *²³* He blotted out every living thing that was on the face of the ground, man and animals and creeping things and birds of the heavens. They were blotted out from the earth. Only Noah was left, and those who were with him in the ark. *²⁴* And the waters prevailed on the earth 150 days.

¹ But God remembered Noah and all the beasts and all the livestock that were with him in the ark. And God made a wind blow over the earth, and the waters subsided. *²* The fountains of the deep and the windows of the heavens were closed, the rain from the heavens was restrained, *³* and the waters receded from the earth continually. At the end of 150 days the waters had abated, *⁴* and in the seventh month, on the seventeenth day of the month, the ark came to rest on the mountains of Ararat. *⁵* And the waters continued to abate until the tenth month; in the tenth month, on the first day of the month, the tops of the mountains were seen.

¹³ In the six hundred and first year, in the first month, the first day of the month, the waters were dried from off the earth. And Noah removed the covering of the ark and looked, and behold, the face of the ground was dry. *¹⁴* In the second month, on the twenty-seventh day of the month, the earth had dried out. *¹⁵* Then God said to Noah, *¹⁶* "Go out from the ark, you and your wife, and your sons and your sons' wives with you. *¹⁷* Bring out with you every living thing that is with you of all flesh—birds and animals and every creeping thing that creeps on the earth—that they may swarm on the earth, and be fruitful and multiply on the earth." *¹⁸* So Noah went out, and his sons and his wife and his sons' wives with him. *¹⁹* Every beast, every creeping thing, and every bird, everything that moves on the earth, went out by families from the ark.

²⁰ Then Noah built an altar to the Lord and took some of every clean animal and some of every clean bird and offered burnt offerings on the altar. ²¹ And when the Lord smelled the pleasing aroma, the Lord said in his heart, "I will never again curse the ground because of man, for the intention of man's heart is evil from his youth. Neither will I ever again strike down every living creature as I have done. ²² While the earth remains, seedtime and harvest, cold and heat, summer and winter, day and night, shall not cease."

¹ And God blessed Noah and his sons and said to them, "Be fruitful and multiply and fill the earth. ⁸ Then God said to Noah and to his sons with him, ⁹ "Behold, I establish my covenant with you and your offspring after you, ¹⁰ and with every living creature that is with you, the birds, the livestock, and every beast of the earth with you, as many as came out of the ark; it is for every beast of the earth. ¹¹ I establish my covenant with you, that never again shall all flesh be cut off by the waters of the flood, and never again shall there be a flood to destroy the earth." ¹² And God said, "This is the sign of the covenant that I make between me and you and every living creature that is with you, for all future generations: ¹³ I have set my bow in the cloud, and it shall be a sign of the covenant between me and the earth.

Discuss: What do these verses teach you about God? What do these verses teach you about your relationship to God?

Pray that God will reveal His truth to you as you read the Scriptures.

Read: Genesis 12:1-4; 15:1-6; 18:1-5,8b-15; 22:1-18; Hebrews 11:8-12; Romans 4:2-3

1 Now the Lord said to Abram, "Go from your country and your kindred and your father's house to the land that I will show you. *2* And I will make of you a great nation, and I will bless you and make your name great, so that you will be a blessing. *3* I will bless those who bless you, and him who dishonors you I will curse, and in you all the families of the earth shall be blessed."*4* So Abram went, as the Lord had told him, and Lot went with him. Abram was seventy-five years old when he departed from Haran.

1 After these things the word of the Lord came to Abram in a vision: "Fear not, Abram, I am your shield; your reward shall be very great." *2* But Abram said, "O Lord God, what will you give me, for I continue childless, and the heir of my house is Eliezer of Damascus?" *3* And Abram said, "Behold, you have given me no offspring, and a member of my household will be my heir." *4* And behold, the word of the Lord came to him: "This man shall not be your heir; your very own son shall be your heir." *5* And he brought him outside and said, "Look toward heaven, and number the stars, if you are able to number them." Then he said to him, "So shall your offspring be." *6* And he believed the Lord, and he counted it to him as righteousness.

¹ And the Lord appeared to him by the oaks of Mamre, as he sat at the door of his tent in the heat of the day. ² He lifted up his eyes and looked, and behold, three men were standing in front of him. When he saw them, he ran from the tent door to meet them and bowed himself to the earth ³ and said, "O Lord, if I have found favor in your sight, do not pass by your servant. ⁴ Let a little water be brought, and wash your feet, and rest yourselves under the tree, ⁵ while I bring a morsel of bread, that you may refresh yourselves, and after that you may pass on—since you have come to your servant." So they said, "Do as you have said." And he stood by them under the tree while they ate.

⁹ They said to him, "Where is Sarah your wife?" And he said, "She is in the tent." ¹⁰ The Lord said, "I will surely return to you about this time next year, and Sarah your wife shall have a son." And Sarah was listening at the tent door behind him. ¹¹ Now Abraham and Sarah were old, advanced in years. The way of women had ceased to be with Sarah. ¹² So Sarah laughed to herself, saying, "After I am worn out, and my lord is old, shall I have pleasure?" ¹³ The Lord said to Abraham, "Why did Sarah laugh and say, 'Shall I indeed bear a child, now that I am old?' ¹⁴ Is anything too hard for the Lord? At the appointed time I will return to you, about this time next year, and Sarah shall have a son." ¹⁵ But Sarah denied it, saying, "I did not laugh," for she was afraid. He said, "No, but you did laugh."

¹ After these things God tested Abraham and said to him, "Abraham!" And he said, "Here I am." ² He said, "Take your son, your only son Isaac, whom you love, and go to the land of Moriah, and offer him there as a burnt offering on one of the mountains of

which I shall tell you." ³ So Abraham rose early in the morning, saddled his donkey, and took two of his young men with him, and his son Isaac. And he cut the wood for the burnt offering and arose and went to the place of which God had told him. ⁴ On the third day Abraham lifted up his eyes and saw the place from afar. ⁵ Then Abraham said to his young men, "Stay here with the donkey; I and the boy will go over there and worship and come again to you." ⁶ And Abraham took the wood of the burnt offering and laid it on Isaac his son. And he took in his hand the fire and the knife. So they went both of them together. ⁷ And Isaac said to his father Abraham, "My father!" And he said, "Here I am, my son." He said, "Behold, the fire and the wood, but where is the lamb for a burnt offering?" ⁸ Abraham said, "God will provide for himself the lamb for a burnt offering, my son." So they went both of them together.

⁹ When they came to the place of which God had told him, Abraham built the altar there and laid the wood in order and bound Isaac his son and laid him on the altar, on top of the wood. ¹⁰ Then Abraham reached out his hand and took the knife to slaughter his son. ¹¹ But the angel of the Lord called to him from heaven and said, "Abraham, Abraham!" And he said, "Here I am." ¹² He said, "Do not lay your hand on the boy or do anything to him, for now I know that you fear God, seeing you have not withheld your son, your only son, from me." ¹³ And Abraham lifted up his eyes and looked, and behold, behind him was a ram, caught in a thicket by his horns. And Abraham went and took the ram and offered it up as a burnt offering instead of his son. ¹⁴ So Abraham called the name of that place, "The Lord will provide"; as it is said to this day, "On the mount of the Lord it shall be provided."

^{15} And the angel of the Lord called to Abraham a second time from heaven ^{16} and said, "By myself I have sworn, declares the Lord, because you have done this and have not withheld your son, your only son, ^{17} I will surely bless you, and I will surely multiply your offspring as the stars of heaven and as the sand that is on the seashore. And your offspring shall possess the gate of his enemies, ^{18} and in your offspring shall all the nations of the earth be blessed, because you have obeyed my voice."

Hebrews

^{8} By faith Abraham obeyed when he was called to go out to a place that he was to receive as an inheritance. And he went out, not knowing where he was going. ^{9} By faith he went to live in the land of promise, as in a foreign land, living in tents with Isaac and Jacob, heirs with him of the same promise. ^{10} For he was looking forward to the city that has foundations, whose designer and builder is God. ^{11} By faith Sarah herself received power to conceive, even when she was past the age, since she considered him faithful who had promised. ^{12} Therefore from one man, and him as good as dead, were born descendants as many as the stars of heaven and as many as the innumerable grains of sand by the seashore.

Romans

^{2} For if Abraham was justified by works, he has something to boast about, but not before God. ^{3} For what does the Scripture say? "Abraham believed God, and it was counted to him as righteousness."

Discuss: What do these verses teach you about God? What do these verses teach you about your relationship to God?

Pray that God will reveal His truth to you as you read the Scriptures.

Read: Genesis 25:19-26; 28:10-22; 32:1-2,22-32; 35:1-7,9-15, 22-26

¹⁹ These are the generations of Isaac, Abraham's son: Abraham fathered Isaac, *²⁰* and Isaac was forty years old when he took Rebekah, the daughter of Bethuel the Aramean of Paddan-aram, the sister of Laban the Aramean, to be his wife. *²¹* And Isaac prayed to the Lord for his wife, because she was barren. And the Lord granted his prayer, and Rebekah his wife conceived. *²²* The children struggled together within her, and she said, "If it is thus, why is this happening to me?" So she went to inquire of the Lord. *²³* And the Lord said to her,

"Two nations are in your womb,
    and two peoples from within you shall be divided;
the one shall be stronger than the other,
    the older shall serve the younger."

²⁴ When her days to give birth were completed, behold, there were twins in her womb. *²⁵* The first came out red, all his body like a hairy cloak, so they called his name Esau. *²⁶* Afterward his brother came out with his hand holding Esau's heel, so his name was called Jacob. Isaac was sixty years old when she bore them.

¹⁰ Jacob left Beersheba and went toward Haran. *¹¹* And he came to a certain place and stayed there that night, because the sun had set. Taking one of the stones of the place, he put it under his head and lay down in that place to sleep. *¹²* And he dreamed, and behold, there was a ladder set up on the earth, and the top of it reached to heaven. And behold, the angels of God were ascending and descending on it! *13* And behold, the Lord stood above it and said, "I am the Lord, the God of Abraham your father and the God of Isaac. The land on which you lie I will give to you and to your offspring. *14* Your offspring shall be like the dust of the earth, and you shall spread abroad to the west and to the east and to the north and to the south, and in you and your offspring shall all the families of the earth be blessed. *15* Behold, I am with you and will keep you wherever you go, and will bring you back to this land. For I will not leave you until I have done what I have promised you." *16* Then Jacob awoke from his sleep and said, "Surely the Lord is in this place, and I did not know it." *17* And he was afraid and said, "How awesome is this place! This is none other than the house of God, and this is the gate of heaven."

18 So early in the morning Jacob took the stone that he had put under his head and set it up for a pillar and poured oil on the top of it. *19* He called the name of that place Bethel, but the name of the city was Luz at the first. *20* Then Jacob made a vow, saying, "If God will be with me and will keep me in this way that I go, and will give me bread to eat and clothing to wear, *21* so that I come again to my father's house in peace, then the Lord shall be my God, *22* and this stone, which I have set up for a pillar, shall be God's house. And of all that you give me I will give a full tenth to you."

1 Jacob went on his way, and the angels of God met him. *2* And when Jacob saw them he said, "This is God's camp!" So he called the name of that place Mahanaim.

22 The same night he arose and took his two wives, his two female servants, and his eleven children, and crossed the ford of the Jabbok. *23* He took them and sent them across the stream, and everything else that he had. *24* And Jacob was left alone. And a man wrestled with him until the breaking of the day. *25* When the man saw that he did not prevail against Jacob, he touched his hip socket, and Jacob's hip was put out of joint as he wrestled with him. *26* Then he said, "Let me go, for the day has broken." But Jacob said, "I will not let you go unless you bless me." *27* And he said to him, "What is your name?" And he said, "Jacob." *28* Then he said, "Your name shall no longer be called Jacob, but Israel, for you have striven with God and with men, and have prevailed." *29* Then Jacob asked him, "Please tell me your name." But he said, "Why is it that you ask my name?" And there he blessed him. *30* So Jacob called the name of the place Peniel, saying, "For I have seen God face to face, and yet my life has been delivered." *31* The sun rose upon him as he passed Penuel, limping because of his hip. *32* Therefore to this day the people of Israel do not eat the sinew of the thigh that is on the hip socket, because he touched the socket of Jacob's hip on the sinew of the thigh.

1 God said to Jacob, "Arise, go up to Bethel and dwell there. Make an altar there to the God who appeared to you when you fled from your brother Esau." *2* So Jacob said to his household and to all who were with him, "Put away the foreign gods that are among you and purify yourselves and change your garments. *3* Then let us arise and go up to Bethel, so that I may make there an altar to the God who answers me in the day of my distress and has been with me wherever I have gone." *4* So they gave to Jacob all the foreign gods that they had, and the rings that were in their ears. Jacob hid them under the terebinth tree that was near Shechem.

⁵ And as they journeyed, a terror from God fell upon the cities that were around them, so that they did not pursue the sons of Jacob. ⁶ And Jacob came to Luz (that is, Bethel), which is in the land of Canaan, he and all the people who were with him, ⁷ and there he built an altar and called the place El-bethel, because there God had revealed himself to him when he fled from his brother.

⁹ God appeared to Jacob again, when he came from Paddan-aram, and blessed him. ¹⁰ And God said to him, "Your name is Jacob; no longer shall your name be called Jacob, but Israel shall be your name." So he called his name Israel. ¹¹ And God said to him, "I am God Almighty: be fruitful and multiply. A nation and a company of nations shall come from you, and kings shall come from your own body. ¹² The land that I gave to Abraham and Isaac I will give to you, and I will give the land to your offspring after you." ¹³ Then God went up from him in the place where he had spoken with him. ¹⁴ And Jacob set up a pillar in the place where he had spoken with him, a pillar of stone. He poured out a drink offering on it and poured oil on it. ¹⁵ So Jacob called the name of the place where God had spoken with him Bethel.

²²ᵇ Now the sons of Jacob were twelve. ²³ The sons of Leah: Reuben (Jacob's firstborn), Simeon, Levi, Judah, Issachar, and Zebulun. ²⁴ The sons of Rachel: Joseph and Benjamin. ²⁵ The sons of Bilhah, Rachel's servant: Dan and Naphtali. ²⁶ The sons of Zilpah, Leah's servant: Gad and Asher. These were the sons of Jacob who were born to him in Paddan-aram.

Discuss: What do these verses teach you about God? What do these verses teach you about your relationship to God?

Pray that God will reveal His truth to you as you read the Scriptures.

Read: Genesis 37:3-4, 12-14, 23-24, 28, 31-33, 36; 41:46-49, 56-57; 42:1-7; 45:1-8; 47:11; Exodus 1:6-13

³ Now Israel loved Joseph more than any other of his sons, because he was the son of his old age. And he made him a robe of many colors. ⁴ But when his brothers saw that their father loved him more than all his brothers, they hated him and could not speak peacefully to him.

¹² Now his brothers went to pasture their father's flock near Shechem. ¹³ And Israel said to Joseph, "Are not your brothers pasturing the flock at Shechem? Come, I will send you to them." And he said to him, "Here I am." ¹⁴ So he said to him, "Go now, see if it is well with your brothers and with the flock, and bring me word." So he sent him from the Valley of Hebron, and he came to Shechem.

²³ So when Joseph came to his brothers, they stripped him of his robe, the robe of many colors that he wore. ²⁴ And they took him and threw him into a pit. The pit was empty; there was no water in it.

²⁸ Then Midianite traders passed by. And they drew Joseph up and lifted him out of the pit, and sold him to the Ishmaelites for twenty shekels of silver. They took Joseph to Egypt.

³¹ Then they took Joseph's robe and slaughtered a goat and dipped the robe in the blood. ³² And they sent the robe of many colors and brought it to their father and said, "This we have found; please identify whether it is your son's robe or not." ³³ And

he identified it and said, "It is my son's robe. A fierce animal has devoured him. Joseph is without doubt torn to pieces."

³⁶ Meanwhile the Midianites had sold him in Egypt to Potiphar, an officer of Pharaoh, the captain of the guard.

⁴⁶ Joseph was thirty years old when he entered the service of Pharaoh king of Egypt. And Joseph went out from the presence of Pharaoh and went through all the land of Egypt. ⁴⁷ During the seven plentiful years the earth produced abundantly, ⁴⁸ and he gathered up all the food of these seven years, which occurred in the land of Egypt, and put the food in the cities. He put in every city the food from the fields around it. ⁴⁹ And Joseph stored up grain in great abundance, like the sand of the sea, until he ceased to measure it, for it could not be measured.

⁵⁶ So when the famine had spread over all the land, Joseph opened all the storehouses and sold to the Egyptians, for the famine was severe in the land of Egypt. ⁵⁷ Moreover, all the earth came to Egypt to Joseph to buy grain, because the famine was severe over all the earth.

¹ When Jacob learned that there was grain for sale in Egypt, he said to his sons, "Why do you look at one another?" ² And he said, "Behold, I have heard that there is grain for sale in Egypt. Go down and buy grain for us there, that we may live and not die." ³ So ten of Joseph's brothers went down to buy grain in Egypt. ⁴ But Jacob did not send Benjamin, Joseph's brother, with his brothers, for he feared that harm might happen to him. ⁵ Thus the sons of Israel came to buy among the others who came, for the famine was in the land of Canaan.

⁶ Now Joseph was governor over the land. He was the one who sold to all the people of the land. And Joseph's brothers came

and bowed themselves before him with their faces to the ground. [7] Joseph saw his brothers and recognized them, but he treated them like strangers and spoke roughly to them. "Where do you come from?" he said. They said, "From the land of Canaan, to buy food."

[1] Then Joseph could not control himself before all those who stood by him. He cried, "Make everyone go out from me." So no one stayed with him when Joseph made himself known to his brothers. [2] And he wept aloud, so that the Egyptians heard it, and the household of Pharaoh heard it. [3] And Joseph said to his brothers, "I am Joseph! Is my father still alive?" But his brothers could not answer him, for they were dismayed at his presence.

[4] So Joseph said to his brothers, "Come near to me, please." And they came near. And he said, "I am your brother, Joseph, whom you sold into Egypt. [5] And now do not be distressed or angry with yourselves because you sold me here, for God sent me before you to preserve life. [6] For the famine has been in the land these two years, and there are yet five years in which there will be neither plowing nor harvest. [7] And God sent me before you to preserve for you a remnant on earth, and to keep alive for you many survivors. [8] So it was not you who sent me here, but God. He has made me a father to Pharaoh, and lord of all his house and ruler over all the land of Egypt.

[11] Then Joseph settled his father and his brothers and gave them a possession in the land of Egypt, in the best of the land, in the land of Rameses, as Pharaoh had commanded.

Exodus

[6] Then Joseph died, and all his brothers and all that generation. [7] But the people of Israel were fruitful and increased greatly;

they multiplied and grew exceedingly strong, so that the land was filled with them.

⁸ Now there arose a new king over Egypt, who did not know Joseph. ⁹ And he said to his people, "Behold, the people of Israel are too many and too mighty for us. ¹⁰ Come, let us deal shrewdly with them, lest they multiply, and, if war breaks out, they join our enemies and fight against us and escape from the land." ¹¹ Therefore they set taskmasters over them to afflict them with heavy burdens. They built for Pharaoh store cities, Pithom and Raamses. ¹² But the more they were oppressed, the more they multiplied and the more they spread abroad. And the Egyptians were in dread of the people of Israel. ¹³ So they ruthlessly made the people of Israel work as slaves

Discuss: What do these verses teach you about God? What do these verses teach you about your relationship to God?

Pray that God will reveal His truth to you as you read the Scriptures.

Read: Exodus 1:22; 2:1-16,21-25; 3:1-14,18-22

²² Then Pharaoh commanded all his people, "Every son that is born to the Hebrews you shall cast into the Nile, but you shall let every daughter live."

¹ Now a man from the house of Levi went and took as his wife a Levite woman. ² The woman conceived and bore a son, and when she saw that he was a fine child, she hid him three months. ³ When she could hide him no longer, she took for him a basket made of bulrushes and daubed it with bitumen and pitch. She put the child in it and placed it among the reeds by the river bank. ⁴ And his sister stood at a distance to know what would be done to him. ⁵ Now the daughter of Pharaoh came down to bathe at the river, while her young women walked beside the river. She saw the basket among the reeds and sent her servant woman, and she took it. ⁶ When she opened it, she saw the child, and behold, the baby was crying. She took pity on him and said, "This is one of the Hebrews' children." ⁷ Then his sister said to Pharaoh's daughter, "Shall I go and call you a nurse from the Hebrew women to nurse the child for you?" ⁸ And Pharaoh's daughter said to her, "Go." So the girl went and called the child's mother. ⁹ And Pharaoh's daughter said to her, "Take this child away and nurse him for me, and I will give you your wages." So the woman took the child and nursed him. ¹⁰ When the child grew older, she brought him to Pharaoh's daughter, and he became her son. She

named him Moses, "Because," she said, "I drew him out of the water."

¹¹ One day, when Moses had grown up, he went out to his people and looked on their burdens, and he saw an Egyptian beating a Hebrew, one of his people. ¹² He looked this way and that, and seeing no one, he struck down the Egyptian and hid him in the sand. ¹³ When he went out the next day, behold, two Hebrews were struggling together. And he said to the man in the wrong, "Why do you strike your companion?" ¹⁴ He answered, "Who made you a prince and a judge over us? Do you mean to kill me as you killed the Egyptian?" Then Moses was afraid, and thought, "Surely the thing is known." ¹⁵ When Pharaoh heard of it, he sought to kill Moses. But Moses fled from Pharaoh and stayed in the land of Midian. And he sat down by a well.¹⁶ Now the priest of Midian had seven daughters, and they came and drew water and filled the troughs to water their father's flock.²¹ And Moses was content to dwell with the man, and he gave Moses his daughter Zipporah. ²² She gave birth to a son, and he called his name Gershom, for he said, "I have been a sojourner in a foreign land."

²³ During those many days the king of Egypt died, and the people of Israel groaned because of their slavery and cried out for help. Their cry for rescue from slavery came up to God. ²⁴ And God heard their groaning, and God remembered his covenant with Abraham, with Isaac, and with Jacob. ²⁵ God saw the people of Israel—and God knew.

¹ Now Moses was keeping the flock of his father-in-law, Jethro, the priest of Midian, and he led his flock to the west side of the wilderness and came to Horeb, the mountain of God. ² And

the angel of the Lord appeared to him in a flame of fire out of the midst of a bush. He looked, and behold, the bush was burning, yet it was not consumed. *3* And Moses said, "I will turn aside to see this great sight, why the bush is not burned." *4* When the Lord saw that he turned aside to see, God called to him out of the bush, "Moses, Moses!" And he said, "Here I am." *5* Then he said, "Do not come near; take your sandals off your feet, for the place on which you are standing is holy ground." *6* And he said, "I am the God of your father, the God of Abraham, the God of Isaac, and the God of Jacob." And Moses hid his face, for he was afraid to look at God.

7 Then the Lord said, "I have surely seen the affliction of my people who are in Egypt and have heard their cry because of their taskmasters. I know their sufferings, *8* and I have come down to deliver them out of the hand of the Egyptians and to bring them up out of that land to a good and broad land, a land flowing with milk and honey, to the place of the Canaanites, the Hittites, the Amorites, the Perizzites, the Hivites, and the Jebusites. *9* And now, behold, the cry of the people of Israel has come to me, and I have also seen the oppression with which the Egyptians oppress them. *10* Come, I will send you to Pharaoh that you may bring my people, the children of Israel, out of Egypt." *11* But Moses said to God, "Who am I that I should go to Pharaoh and bring the children of Israel out of Egypt?" *12* He said, "But I will be with you, and this shall be the sign for you, that I have sent you: when you have brought the people out of Egypt, you shall serve God on this mountain."

¹³ Then Moses said to God, "If I come to the people of Israel and say to them, 'The God of your fathers has sent me to you,' and they ask me, 'What is his name?' what shall I say to them?" ¹⁴ God said to Moses, "I am who I am." And he said, "Say this to the people of Israel, 'I am has sent me to you.'"

¹⁸ And they will listen to your voice, and you and the elders of Israel shall go to the king of Egypt and say to him, 'The Lord, the God of the Hebrews, has met with us; and now, please let us go a three days' journey into the wilderness, that we may sacrifice to the Lord our God.' ¹⁹ But I know that the king of Egypt will not let you go unless compelled by a mighty hand. ²⁰ So I will stretch out my hand and strike Egypt with all the wonders that I will do in it; after that he will let you go. ²¹ And I will give this people favor in the sight of the Egyptians; and when you go, you shall not go empty, ²² but each woman shall ask of her neighbor, and any woman who lives in her house, for silver and gold jewelry, and for clothing. You shall put them on your sons and on your daughters. So you shall plunder the Egyptians."

Discuss: What do these verses teach you about God? What do these verses teach you about your relationship to God?

Joy
Light the second purple candle

Go your way. Eat the fat and drink sweet wine and send portions to anyone who has nothing ready, for this day is holy to our Lord. And do not be grieved, for the joy of the Lord is your strength.
Nehemiah 8:10

The Israelites wept at the reading of the Law, recognizing that they fell short of God's standards. But God, through the law, also offered hope and opportunity for reconciliation. God promised a Redeemer for those guilty under the law, a Savior who would emerge from the lineage of David. With this hope they were to rejoice and share with others.

Suggestions for the week

· Sing *Joy To The World*
· Meditate on the joy of knowing and being in a right relationship with God.
· Thank Him that Scripture is readily available to learn who He is and how great is His love for you.
· Thank Him that His ways are for our good and Jesus was sent as the fulfillment of the Law.

Pray that God will reveal His truth to you as you read the Scriptures.

Read: Exodus 4:19-23; 6:2-8; 10-12; 7:1-7; 10:1-2; 11:10; 12:1-13, 17, 29-36

¹⁹ And the Lord said to Moses in Midian, "Go back to Egypt, for all the men who were seeking your life are dead." ²⁰ So Moses took his wife and his sons and had them ride on a donkey, and went back to the land of Egypt. And Moses took the staff of God in his hand.

²¹ And the Lord said to Moses, "When you go back to Egypt, see that you do before Pharaoh all the miracles that I have put in your power. But I will harden his heart, so that he will not let the people go. ²² Then you shall say to Pharaoh, 'Thus says the Lord, Israel is my firstborn son, ²³ and I say to you, "Let my son go that he may serve me." If you refuse to let him go, behold, I will kill your firstborn son.'"

² God spoke to Moses and said to him, "I am the Lord. ³ I appeared to Abraham, to Isaac, and to Jacob, as God Almighty, but by my name the Lord I did not make myself known to them. ⁴ I also established my covenant with them to give them the land of Canaan, the land in which they lived as sojourners. ⁵ Moreover, I have heard the groaning of the people of Israel whom the Egyptians hold as slaves, and I have remembered my covenant. ⁶ Say therefore to the people of Israel, 'I am the Lord, and I will bring you out from under the burdens of the Egyptians, and I will deliver you from slavery to them, and I will redeem you with an outstretched arm and with great acts of judgment. ⁷ I will take

you to be my people, and I will be your God, and you shall know that I am the Lord your God, who has brought you out from under the burdens of the Egyptians. *8* I will bring you into the land that I swore to give to Abraham, to Isaac, and to Jacob. I will give it to you for a possession. I am the Lord.'"

10 So the Lord said to Moses, *11* "Go in, tell Pharaoh king of Egypt to let the people of Israel go out of his land." *12* But Moses said to the Lord, "Behold, the people of Israel have not listened to me. How then shall Pharaoh listen to me, for I am of uncircumcised lips?"

1 And the Lord said to Moses, "See, I have made you like God to Pharaoh, and your brother Aaron shall be your prophet. *2* You shall speak all that I command you, and your brother Aaron shall tell Pharaoh to let the people of Israel go out of his land. *3* But I will harden Pharaoh's heart, and though I multiply my signs and wonders in the land of Egypt, *4* Pharaoh will not listen to you. Then I will lay my hand on Egypt and bring my hosts, my people the children of Israel, out of the land of Egypt by great acts of judgment. *5* The Egyptians shall know that I am the Lord, when I stretch out my hand against Egypt and bring out the people of Israel from among them." *6* Moses and Aaron did so; they did just as the Lord commanded them. *7* Now Moses was eighty years old, and Aaron eighty-three years old, when they spoke to Pharaoh.

1 Then the Lord said to Moses, "Go in to Pharaoh, for I have hardened his heart and the heart of his servants, that I may show these signs of mine among them, *2* and that you may tell in the hearing of your son and of your grandson how I have dealt harshly with the Egyptians and what signs I have done among them, that you may know that I am the Lord."

¹⁰ Moses and Aaron did all these wonders before Pharaoh, and the Lord hardened Pharaoh's heart, and he did not let the people of Israel go out of his land.

¹ The Lord said to Moses and Aaron in the land of Egypt, ² "This month shall be for you the beginning of months. It shall be the first month of the year for you. ³ Tell all the congregation of Israel that on the tenth day of this month every man shall take a lamb according to their fathers' houses, a lamb for a household. ⁴ And if the household is too small for a lamb, then he and his nearest neighbor shall take according to the number of persons; according to what each can eat you shall make your count for the lamb. ⁵ Your lamb shall be without blemish, a male a year old. You may take it from the sheep or from the goats, ⁶ and you shall keep it until the fourteenth day of this month, when the whole assembly of the congregation of Israel shall kill their lambs at twilight.

⁷ "Then they shall take some of the blood and put it on the two doorposts and the lintel of the houses in which they eat it. ⁸ They shall eat the flesh that night, roasted on the fire; with unleavened bread and bitter herbs they shall eat it. ⁹ Do not eat any of it raw or boiled in water, but roasted, its head with its legs and its inner parts. ¹⁰ And you shall let none of it remain until the morning; anything that remains until the morning you shall burn. ¹¹ In this manner you shall eat it: with your belt fastened, your sandals on your feet, and your staff in your hand. And you shall eat it in haste. It is the Lord's Passover. ¹² For I will pass through

the land of Egypt that night, and I will strike all the firstborn in the land of Egypt, both man and beast; and on all the gods of Egypt I will execute judgments: I am the Lord. *13* The blood shall be a sign for you, on the houses where you are. And when I see the blood, I will pass over you, and no plague will befall you to destroy you, when I strike the land of Egypt.

17 And you shall observe the Feast of Unleavened Bread, for on this very day I brought your hosts out of the land of Egypt. Therefore you shall observe this day, throughout your generations, as a statute forever.

29 At midnight the Lord struck down all the firstborn in the land of Egypt, from the firstborn of Pharaoh who sat on his throne to the firstborn of the captive who was in the dungeon, and all the firstborn of the livestock. *30* And Pharaoh rose up in the night, he and all his servants and all the Egyptians. And there was a great cry in Egypt, for there was not a house where someone was not dead. *31* Then he summoned Moses and Aaron by night and said, "Up, go out from among my people, both you and the people of Israel; and go, serve the Lord, as you have said. *32* Take your flocks and your herds, as you have said, and be gone, and bless me also!"

33 The Egyptians were urgent with the people to send them out of the land in haste. For they said, "We shall all be dead." *34* So the people took their dough before it was leavened, their kneading bowls being bound up in their cloaks on their shoulders. *35* The people of Israel had also done as Moses told them, for they had asked the Egyptians for silver and gold jewelry and for clothing. *36* And the Lord had given the people favor in the sight of the

Egyptians, so that they let them have what they asked. Thus they plundered the Egyptians.

Discuss: What do these verses teach you about God? What do these verses teach you about your relationship to God?

Pray that God will reveal His truth to you as you read the Scriptures.

Read: Exodus 12:37-42, 50-51; 19:1-6; 20:1-17; 24:7-8

[37] And the people of Israel journeyed from Rameses to Succoth, about six hundred thousand men on foot, besides women and children. [38] A mixed multitude also went up with them, and very much livestock, both flocks and herds. [39] And they baked unleavened cakes of the dough that they had brought out of Egypt, for it was not leavened, because they were thrust out of Egypt and could not wait, nor had they prepared any provisions for themselves.

[40] The time that the people of Israel lived in Egypt was 430 years. [41] At the end of 430 years, on that very day, all the hosts of the Lord went out from the land of Egypt. [42] It was a night of watching by the Lord, to bring them out of the land of Egypt; so this same night is a night of watching kept to the Lord by all the people of Israel throughout their generations.

[50] All the people of Israel did just as the Lord commanded Moses and Aaron. [51] And on that very day the Lord brought the people of Israel out of the land of Egypt by their hosts.

[1] On the third new moon after the people of Israel had gone out of the land of Egypt, on that day they came into the wilderness of Sinai. [2] They set out from Rephidim and came into the wilderness of Sinai, and they encamped in the wilderness. There Israel encamped before the mountain, [3] while Moses went up to God. The Lord called to him out of the mountain, saying, "Thus

you shall say to the house of Jacob, and tell the people of Israel: [4] You yourselves have seen what I did to the Egyptians, and how I bore you on eagles' wings and brought you to myself. [5] Now therefore, if you will indeed obey my voice and keep my covenant, you shall be my treasured possession among all peoples, for all the earth is mine; [6] and you shall be to me a kingdom of priests and a holy nation. These are the words that you shall speak to the people of Israel."

[20] And God spoke all these words, saying,

[2] "I am the Lord your God, who brought you out of the land of Egypt, out of the house of slavery.

[3] "You shall have no other gods before me.

[4] "You shall not make for yourself a carved image, or any likeness of anything that is in heaven above, or that is in the earth beneath, or that is in the water under the earth. [5] You shall not bow down to them or serve them, for I the Lord your God am a jealous God, visiting the iniquity of the fathers on the children to the third and the fourth generation of those who hate me, [6] but showing steadfast love to thousands of those who love me and keep my commandments.

[7] "You shall not take the name of the Lord your God in vain, for the Lord will not hold him guiltless who takes his name in vain.

[8] "Remember the Sabbath day, to keep it holy. [9] Six days you shall labor, and do all your work, [10] but the seventh day is a Sabbath to the Lord your God. On it you shall not do any work, you, or your son, or your daughter, your male servant, or your female servant, or your livestock, or the sojourner who is within your gates. [11] For in six days the Lord made heaven and earth, the sea,

and all that is in them, and rested on the seventh day. Therefore the Lord blessed the Sabbath day and made it holy.

[12] "Honor your father and your mother, that your days may be long in the land that the Lord your God is giving you.

[13] "You shall not murder.

[14] "You shall not commit adultery.

[15] "You shall not steal.

[16] "You shall not bear false witness against your neighbor.

[17] "You shall not covet your neighbor's house; you shall not covet your neighbor's wife, or his male servant, or his female servant, or his ox, or his donkey, or anything that is your neighbor's."

[7] Then he took the Book of the Covenant and read it in the hearing of the people. And they said, "All that the Lord has spoken we will do, and we will be obedient." [8] And Moses took the blood and threw it on the people and said, "Behold the blood of the covenant that the Lord has made with you in accordance with all these words."

Discuss: What do these verses teach you about God? What do these verses teach you about your relationship to God?

Pray that God will reveal His truth to you as you read the Scriptures.

Read: Joshua 1:1-2, 8-9, 2:1-21; 6:1-5, 12-17, 20, 22-25

¹ After the death of Moses the servant of the Lord, the Lord said to Joshua the son of Nun, Moses' assistant, ² "Moses my servant is dead. Now therefore arise, go over this Jordan, you and all this people, into the land that I am giving to them, to the people of Israel. ⁸ This Book of the Law shall not depart from your mouth, but you shall meditate on it day and night, so that you may be careful to do according to all that is written in it. For then you will make your way prosperous, and then you will have good success. ⁹ Have I not commanded you? Be strong and courageous. Do not be frightened, and do not be dismayed, for the Lord your God is with you wherever you go."

¹ And Joshua the son of Nun sent two men secretly from Shittim as spies, saying, "Go, view the land, especially Jericho." And they went and came into the house of a prostitute whose name was Rahab and lodged there. ² And it was told to the king of Jericho, "Behold, men of Israel have come here tonight to search out the land." ³ Then the king of Jericho sent to Rahab, saying, "Bring out the men who have come to you, who entered your house, for they have come to search out all the land." ⁴ But the woman had taken the two men and hidden them. And she said, "True, the men came to me, but I did not know where they were from. ⁵ And when the gate was about to be closed at dark, the men went out. I do not know where the men went. Pursue them

quickly, for you will overtake them." [6] But she had brought them up to the roof and hid them with the stalks of flax that she had laid in order on the roof. [7] So the men pursued after them on the way to the Jordan as far as the fords. And the gate was shut as soon as the pursuers had gone out.

[8] Before the men lay down, she came up to them on the roof [9] and said to the men, "I know that the Lord has given you the land, and that the fear of you has fallen upon us, and that all the inhabitants of the land melt away before you. [10] For we have heard how the Lord dried up the water of the Red Sea before you when you came out of Egypt, and what you did to the two kings of the Amorites who were beyond the Jordan, to Sihon and Og, whom you devoted to destruction. [11] And as soon as we heard it, our hearts melted, and there was no spirit left in any man because of you, for the Lord your God, he is God in the heavens above and on the earth beneath. [12] Now then, please swear to me by the Lord that, as I have dealt kindly with you, you also will deal kindly with my father's house, and give me a sure sign [13] that you will save alive my father and mother, my brothers and sisters, and all who belong to them, and deliver our lives from death." [14] And the men said to her, "Our life for yours even to death! If you do not tell this business of ours, then when the Lord gives us the land we will deal kindly and faithfully with you."

[15] Then she let them down by a rope through the window, for her house was built into the city wall, so that she lived in the wall. [16] And she said to them, "Go into the hills, or the pursuers will encounter you, and hide there three days until the pursuers have returned. Then afterward you may go your way." [17] The men said to her, "We will be guiltless with respect to this oath of yours that

you have made us swear. *18* Behold, when we come into the land, you shall tie this scarlet cord in the window through which you let us down, and you shall gather into your house your father and mother, your brothers, and all your father's household. *19* Then if anyone goes out of the doors of your house into the street, his blood shall be on his own head, and we shall be guiltless. But if a hand is laid on anyone who is with you in the house, his blood shall be on our head. *20* But if you tell this business of ours, then we shall be guiltless with respect to your oath that you have made us swear." *21* And she said, "According to your words, so be it." Then she sent them away, and they departed. And she tied the scarlet cord in the window.

1 Now Jericho was shut up inside and outside because of the people of Israel. None went out, and none came in. *2* And the Lord said to Joshua, "See, I have given Jericho into your hand, with its king and mighty men of valor. *3* You shall march around the city, all the men of war going around the city once. Thus shall you do for six days. *4* Seven priests shall bear seven trumpets of rams' horns before the ark. On the seventh day you shall march around the city seven times, and the priests shall blow the trumpets. *5* And when they make a long blast with the ram's horn, when you hear the sound of the trumpet, then all the people shall shout with a great shout, and the wall of the city will fall down flat, and the people shall go up, everyone straight before him."

12 Then Joshua rose early in the morning, and the priests took up the ark of the Lord. *13* And the seven priests bearing the seven trumpets of rams' horns before the ark of the Lord walked on, and they blew the trumpets continually. And the armed men were walking before them, and the rear guard was walking after the ark of the Lord, while the trumpets blew continually. *14* And the second day they marched around the city once, and returned into the camp. So they did for six days.

15 On the seventh day they rose early, at the dawn of day, and marched around the city in the same manner seven times. It was only on that day that they marched around the city seven times. *16* And at the seventh time, when the priests had blown the trumpets, Joshua said to the people, "Shout, for the Lord has given you the city. *17* And the city and all that is within it shall be devoted to the Lord for destruction. Only Rahab the prostitute and all who are with her in her house shall live, because she hid the messengers whom we sent. *20* So the people shouted, and the trumpets were blown. As soon as the people heard the sound of the trumpet, the people shouted a great shout, and the wall fell down flat, so that the people went up into the city, every man straight before him, and they captured the city.*22* But to the two men who had spied out the land, Joshua said, "Go into the prostitute's house and bring out from there the woman and all who belong to her, as you swore to her." *23* So the young men who had been spies went in and brought out Rahab and her father and mother and brothers and all who belonged to her. And they brought all her relatives and put them outside the camp of Israel. *24* And they burned the city with fire, and everything in it. Only the silver and gold, and the vessels of bronze and of iron, they put into the treasury of the house of the Lord. *25* But Rahab the prostitute and her father's household and all who belonged to her, Joshua saved alive. And she has lived in Israel to this day, because she hid the messengers whom Joshua sent to spy out Jericho.

Discuss: What do these verses teach you about God? What do these verses teach you about your relationship to God?

Second Wednesday of Advent

Pray that God will reveal His truth to you as you read the Scriptures.

Read: Ruth 1:1, 3-6, 8-9, 14, 16-18, 22; 2:1-23; 4:1,3-6, 13-17

^{1} In the days when the judges ruled there was a famine in the land, and a man of Bethlehem in Judah went to sojourn in the country of Moab, he and his wife and his two sons. ^{3} But Elimelech, the husband of Naomi, died, and she was left with her two sons. ^{4} These took Moabite wives; the name of the one was Orpah and the name of the other Ruth. They lived there about ten years, ^{5} and both Mahlon and Chilion died, so that the woman was left without her two sons and her husband.

^{6} Then she arose with her daughters-in-law to return from the country of Moab, for she had heard in the fields of Moab that the Lord had visited his people and given them food. ^{8} But Naomi said to her two daughters-in-law, "Go, return each of you to her mother's house. May the Lord deal kindly with you, as you have dealt with the dead and with me. ^{9} The Lord grant that you may find rest, each of you in the house of her husband!" Then she kissed them, and they lifted up their voices and wept. ^{14} Then they lifted up their voices and wept again. And Orpah kissed her mother-in-law, but Ruth clung to her.

^{16} But Ruth said, "Do not urge me to leave you or to return from following you. For where you go I will go, and where you lodge I will lodge. Your people shall be my people, and your God my God. *17* Where you die I will die, and there will I be buried. May the Lord do so to me and more also if anything but death parts me from you." *18* And when Naomi saw that she was determined to go with her, she said no more.

22 So Naomi returned, and Ruth the Moabite her daughter-in-law with her, who returned from the country of Moab. And they came to Bethlehem at the beginning of barley harvest.

1 Now Naomi had a relative of her husband's, a worthy man of the clan of Elimelech, whose name was Boaz. *2* And Ruth the Moabite said to Naomi, "Let me go to the field and glean among the ears of grain after him in whose sight I shall find favor." And she said to her, "Go, my daughter." *3* So she set out and went and gleaned in the field after the reapers, and she happened to come to the part of the field belonging to Boaz, who was of the clan of Elimelech. *4* And behold, Boaz came from Bethlehem. And he said to the reapers, "The Lord be with you!" And they answered, "The Lord bless you." *5* Then Boaz said to his young man who was in charge of the reapers, "Whose young woman is this?" *6* And the servant who was in charge of the reapers answered, "She is the young Moabite woman, who came back with Naomi from the country of Moab. *7* She said, 'Please let me glean and gather among the sheaves after the reapers.' So she came, and she has continued from early morning until now, except for a short rest."

8 Then Boaz said to Ruth, "Now, listen, my daughter, do not go to glean in another field or leave this one, but keep close to my young women. *9* Let your eyes be on the field that they are reaping, and go after them. Have I not charged the young men not to touch you? And when you are thirsty, go to the vessels and drink what the young men have drawn." *10* Then she fell on her face, bowing to the ground, and said to him, "Why have I found favor in your eyes, that you should take notice of me, since I am a foreigner?" *11* But Boaz answered her, "All that you have done for your mother-in-law since the death of your husband has been fully told to me, and how you left your father and mother and your native land and came to a people that you did not know before. *12* The Lord repay you for what you have done, and a full reward be given you by the Lord, the God of Israel, under whose wings you have come to take refuge!" *13* Then she said, "I have found favor in your eyes, my lord, for you have comforted me and spoken kindly to your servant, though I am not one of your servants."

14 And at mealtime Boaz said to her, "Come here and eat some bread and dip your morsel in the wine." So she sat beside the reapers, and he passed to her roasted grain. And she ate until she was satisfied, and she had some left over. *15* When she rose to glean, Boaz instructed his young men, saying, "Let her glean even among the sheaves, and do not reproach her. *16* And also pull out some from the bundles for her and leave it for her to glean, and do not rebuke her."

17 So she gleaned in the field until evening. Then she beat out what she had gleaned, and it was about an ephah of barley. *18* And she took it up and went into the city. Her mother-in-law saw what she had gleaned. She also brought out and gave her what food she had left over after being satisfied. [19] And her mother-in-law said to her, "Where did you glean today? And where have you worked? Blessed be the man who took notice of you." So she told her mother-in-law with whom she had worked and said, "The man's name with whom I worked today is Boaz." [20] And Naomi said to her daughter-in-law, "May he be blessed by the Lord, whose kindness has not forsaken the living or the dead!" Naomi also said to her, "The man is a close relative of ours, one of our redeemers." [21] And Ruth the Moabite said, "Besides, he said to me, 'You shall keep close by my young men until they have finished all my harvest.'" [22] And Naomi said to Ruth, her daughter-in-law, "It is good, my daughter, that you go out with his young women, lest in another field you be assaulted." [23] So she kept close to the young women of Boaz, gleaning until the end of the barley and wheat harvests. And she lived with her mother-in-law.

[1] Now Boaz had gone up to the gate and sat down there. And behold, the redeemer, of whom Boaz had spoken, came by. So Boaz said, "Turn aside, friend; sit down here." And he turned aside and sat down [3] Then he said to the redeemer, "Naomi, who has come back from the country of Moab, is selling the parcel of land that belonged to our relative Elimelech. [4] So I thought I would tell you of it and say, 'Buy it in the presence of those sitting here and in the presence of the elders of my people.' If you will redeem it, redeem it. But if you will not, tell me, that I may know, for there is no one besides you to redeem it, and I come after you." And he said, "I will redeem it." [5] Then Boaz said, "The day you buy the field from the hand of Naomi, you also acquire Ruth the Moabite, the widow of the dead, in order to perpetuate the

name of the dead in his inheritance." ⁶ Then the redeemer said, "I cannot redeem it for myself, lest I impair my own inheritance. Take my right of redemption yourself, for I cannot redeem it."

¹³ So Boaz took Ruth, and she became his wife. And he went in to her, and the Lord gave her conception, and she bore a son. ¹⁴ Then the women said to Naomi, "Blessed be the Lord, who has not left you this day without a redeemer, and may his name be renowned in Israel! ¹⁵ He shall be to you a restorer of life and a nourisher of your old age, for your daughter-in-law who loves you, who is more to you than seven sons, has given birth to him." ¹⁶ Then Naomi took the child and laid him on her lap and became his nurse. ¹⁷ And the women of the neighborhood gave him a name, saying, "A son has been born to Naomi." They named him Obed. He was the father of Jesse, the father of David.

Discuss: What do these verses teach you about God? What do these verses teach you about your relationship to God?

Pray that God will reveal His truth to you as you read the Scriptures.

Read: 1 Samuel 3:20-21; 8:1,3-9; 9:17; 10:1; 13:1,13-14; 15:22-23; 16:1,6-7,11-16,18-19,21

_20_ And all Israel from Dan to Beersheba knew that Samuel was established as a prophet of the Lord. _21_ And the Lord appeared again at Shiloh, for the Lord revealed himself to Samuel at Shiloh by the word of the Lord.

_1_ When Samuel became old, he made his sons judges over Israel. _3_ Yet his sons did not walk in his ways but turned aside after gain. They took bribes and perverted justice.

_4_ Then all the elders of Israel gathered together and came to Samuel at Ramah _5_ and said to him, "Behold, you are old and your sons do not walk in your ways. Now appoint for us a king to judge us like all the nations." _6_ But the thing displeased Samuel when they said, "Give us a king to judge us." And Samuel prayed to the Lord. _7_ And the Lord said to Samuel, "Obey the voice of the people in all that they say to you, for they have not rejected you, but they have rejected me from being king over them. _8_ According to all the deeds that they have done, from the day I brought them up out of Egypt even to this day, forsaking me and serving other gods, so they are also doing to you. _9_ Now then, obey their voice; only you shall solemnly warn them and show them the ways of the king who shall reign over them."

_17_ When Samuel saw Saul, the Lord told him, "Here is the man of whom I spoke to you! He it is who shall restrain my people."

¹ Then Samuel took a flask of oil and poured it on his head and kissed him and said, "Has not the Lord anointed you to be prince over his people Israel? And you shall reign over the people of the Lord and you will save them from the hand of their surrounding enemies. And this shall be the sign to you that the Lord has anointed you to be prince over his heritage.

¹ Saul was thirty years old when he became king, and he reigned over Israel forty- two years.[NIV]

¹³ And Samuel said to Saul, "You have done foolishly. You have not kept the command of the Lord your God, with which he commanded you. For then the Lord would have established your kingdom over Israel forever. ¹⁴ But now your kingdom shall not continue. The Lord has sought out a man after his own heart, and the Lord has commanded him to be prince over his people, because you have not kept what the Lord commanded you."

²² And Samuel said,"Has the Lord as great delight in burnt offerings and sacrifices, as in obeying the voice of the Lord? Behold, to obey is better than sacrifice, and to listen than the fat of rams.

²³ For rebellion is as the sin of divination, and presumption is as iniquity and idolatry. Because you have rejected the word of the Lord, he has also rejected you from being king."

¹ The Lord said to Samuel, "How long will you grieve over Saul, since I have rejected him from being king over Israel? Fill your horn with oil, and go. I will send you to Jesse the

Bethlehemite, for I have provided for myself a king among his sons."

⁶ When they came, he looked on Eliab and thought, "Surely the Lord's anointed is before him." ⁷ But the Lord said to Samuel, "Do not look on his appearance or on the height of his stature, because I have rejected him. For the Lord sees not as man sees: man looks on the outward appearance, but the Lord looks on the heart."

¹¹ Then Samuel said to Jesse, "Are all your sons here?" And he said, "There remains yet the youngest, but behold, he is keeping the sheep." And Samuel said to Jesse, "Send and get him, for we will not sit down till he comes here." ¹² And he sent and brought him in. Now he was ruddy and had beautiful eyes and was handsome. And the Lord said, "Arise, anoint him, for this is he." ¹³ Then Samuel took the horn of oil and anointed him in the midst of his brothers. And the Spirit of the Lord rushed upon David from that day forward. And Samuel rose up and went to Ramah.

¹⁴ Now the Spirit of the Lord departed from Saul, and a harmful spirit from the Lord tormented him. ¹⁵ And Saul's servants said to him, "Behold now, a harmful spirit from God is tormenting you. ¹⁶ Let our lord now command your servants who are before you to seek out a man who is skillful in playing the lyre, and when the harmful spirit from God is upon you, he will play it, and you will be well."

¹⁸ One of the young men answered, "Behold, I have seen a son of Jesse the Bethlehemite, who is skillful in playing, a man of valor, a man of war, prudent in speech, and a man of good presence, and the Lord is with him." ¹⁹ Therefore Saul sent

messengers to Jesse and said, "Send me David your son, who is with the sheep."

²¹ And David came to Saul and entered his service. And Saul loved him greatly, and he became his armor-bearer.

Discuss: What do these verses teach you about God? What do these verses teach you about your relationship to God?

Second Friday of Advent

Pray that God will reveal His truth to you as you read the Scriptures.

Read: 1 Samuel 17:1,4,10-11,26,28-29,31,36-37,45,48-50; 18:12-16; 19:1-2; 20:1,32-34; 21:1,7, 10; 22:6-18

¹ Now the Philistines gathered their armies for battle. ⁴ And there came out from the camp of the Philistines a champion named Goliath of Gath, whose height was six cubits and a span. ¹⁰ And the Philistine said, "I defy the ranks of Israel this day. Give me a man, that we may fight together." ¹¹ When Saul and all Israel heard these words of the Philistine, they were dismayed and greatly afraid.

²⁶ And David said to the men who stood by him, "What shall be done for the man who kills this Philistine and takes away the reproach from Israel? For who is this uncircumcised Philistine, that he should defy the armies of the living God?" ²⁸ Now Eliab his eldest brother heard when he spoke to the men. And Eliab's anger was kindled against David, and he said, "Why have you come down? And with whom have you left those few sheep in the wilderness? I know your presumption and the evil of your heart, for you have come down to see the battle." ²⁹ And David said, "What have I done now? Was it not but a word?" ³¹ When the words that David spoke were heard, they repeated them before Saul, and he sent for him. ³⁶ Your servant has struck down both lions and bears, and this uncircumcised Philistine shall be like one of them, for he has defied the armies of the living God." ³⁷ And David said, "The Lord who delivered me from the paw of the lion and from the

paw of the bear will deliver me from the hand of this Philistine." And Saul said to David, "Go, and the Lord be with you!"

⁴⁵ Then David said to the Philistine, "You come to me with a sword and with a spear and with a javelin, but I come to you in the name of the Lord of hosts, the God of the armies of Israel, whom you have defied. ⁴⁸ When the Philistine arose and came and drew near to meet David, David ran quickly toward the battle line to meet the Philistine. ⁴⁹ And David put his hand in his bag and took out a stone and slung it and struck the Philistine on his forehead. The stone sank into his forehead, and he fell on his face to the ground.

⁵⁰ So David prevailed over the Philistine with a sling and with a stone, and struck the Philistine and killed him. There was no sword in the hand of David.

¹² Saul was afraid of David because the Lord was with him but had departed from Saul. ¹³ So Saul removed him from his presence and made him a commander of a thousand. And he went out and came in before the people. ¹⁴ And David had success in all his undertakings, for the Lord was with him. ¹⁵ And when Saul saw that he had great success, he stood in fearful awe of him. ¹⁶ But all Israel and Judah loved David, for he went out and came in before them.

¹ And Saul spoke to Jonathan his son and to all his servants, that they should kill David. But Jonathan, Saul's son, delighted much in David. ² And Jonathan told David, "Saul my father seeks to kill you. Therefore be on your guard in the morning. Stay in a secret place and hide yourself.

1 Then David fled from Naioth in Ramah and came and said before Jonathan, "What have I done? What is my guilt? And what is my sin before your father, that he seeks my life?"

32 Then Jonathan answered Saul his father, "Why should he be put to death? What has he done?" *33* But Saul hurled his spear at him to strike him. So Jonathan knew that his father was determined to put David to death. *34* And Jonathan rose from the table in fierce anger and ate no food the second day of the month, for he was grieved for David, because his father had disgraced him.

1 Then David came to Nob to Ahimelech the priest. And Ahimelech came to meet David trembling and said to him, "Why are you alone, and no one with you?" *7* Now a certain man of the servants of Saul was there that day, detained before the Lord. His name was Doeg the Edomite, the chief of Saul's herdsmen.

10 And David rose and fled that day from Saul and went to Achish the king of Gath.

6 Now Saul heard that David was discovered, and the men who were with him. Saul was sitting at Gibeah under the tamarisk tree on the height with his spear in his hand, and all his servants were standing about him. *7* And Saul said to his servants who stood about him, "Hear now, people of Benjamin; will the son of Jesse give every one of you fields and vineyards, will he make you all commanders of thousands and commanders of hundreds, *8* that all of you have conspired against me? No one discloses to me when my son makes a covenant with the son of Jesse. None of you is sorry for me or discloses to me that my son has stirred up my servant against me, to lie in wait, as at this day." *9* Then answered Doeg the Edomite, who stood by the servants of Saul, "I saw the son of Jesse coming to Nob, to Ahimelech the son of

Ahitub, [10] and he inquired of the Lord for him and gave him provisions and gave him the sword of Goliath the Philistine."

[11] Then the king sent to summon Ahimelech the priest, the son of Ahitub, and all his father's house, the priests who were at Nob, and all of them came to the king. [12] And Saul said, "Hear now, son of Ahitub." And he answered, "Here I am, my lord." [13] And Saul said to him, "Why have you conspired against me, you and the son of Jesse, in that you have given him bread and a sword and have inquired of God for him, so that he has risen against me, to lie in wait, as at this day?" [14] Then Ahimelech answered the king, "And who among all your servants is so faithful as David, who is the king's son-in-law, and captain over your bodyguard, and honored in your house? [15] Is today the first time that I have inquired of God for him? No! Let not the king impute anything to his servant or to all the house of my father, for your servant has known nothing of all this, much or little." [16] And the king said, "You shall surely die, Ahimelech, you and all your father's house." [17] And the king said to the guard who stood about him, "Turn and kill the priests of the Lord, because their hand also is with David, and they knew that he fled and did not disclose it to me." But the servants of the king would not put out their hand to strike the priests of the Lord. [18] Then the king said to Doeg, "You turn and strike the priests." And Doeg the Edomite turned and struck down the priests, and he killed on that day eighty-five persons who wore the linen ephod.

Discuss: What do these verses teach you about God? What do these verses teach you about your relationship to God?

Second Saturday of Advent

Pray that God will reveal His truth to you as you read the Scriptures.

Read: 1 Samuel 23:14; 24:1-11,16-22; 2 Samuel 5:1-5; 1 Kings 2:1-4; Acts 13:16-23

14 And David remained in the strongholds in the wilderness, in the hill country of the wilderness of Ziph. And Saul sought him every day, but God did not give him into his hand.

1 When Saul returned from following the Philistines, he was told, "Behold, David is in the wilderness of Engedi." *2* Then Saul took three thousand chosen men out of all Israel and went to seek David and his men in front of the Wildgoats' Rocks. *3* And he came to the sheepfolds by the way, where there was a cave, and Saul went in to relieve himself. Now David and his men were sitting in the innermost parts of the cave. *4* And the men of David said to him, "Here is the day of which the Lord said to you, 'Behold, I will give your enemy into your hand, and you shall do to him as it shall seem good to you.'" Then David arose and stealthily cut off a corner of Saul's robe. *5* And afterward David's heart struck him, because he had cut off a corner of Saul's robe. *6* He said to his men, "The Lord forbid that I should do this thing to my lord, the Lord's anointed, to put out my hand against him, seeing he is the Lord's anointed." *7* So David persuaded his men with these words and did not permit them to attack Saul. And Saul rose up and left the cave and went on his way.

⁸ Afterward David also arose and went out of the cave, and called after Saul, "My lord the king!" And when Saul looked behind him, David bowed with his face to the earth and paid homage. ⁹ And David said to Saul, "Why do you listen to the words of men who say, 'Behold, David seeks your harm'? ¹⁰ Behold, this day your eyes have seen how the Lord gave you today into my hand in the cave. And some told me to kill you, but I spared you. I said, 'I will not put out my hand against my lord, for he is the Lord's anointed.' ¹¹ See, my father, see the corner of your robe in my hand. For by the fact that I cut off the corner of your robe and did not kill you, you may know and see that there is no wrong or treason in my hands. I have not sinned against you, though you hunt my life to take it.

¹⁶ As soon as David had finished speaking these words to Saul, Saul said, "Is this your voice, my son David?" And Saul lifted up his voice and wept. ¹⁷ He said to David, "You are more righteous than I, for you have repaid me good, whereas I have repaid you evil. ¹⁸ And you have declared this day how you have dealt well with me, in that you did not kill me when the Lord put me into your hands. ¹⁹ For if a man finds his enemy, will he let him go away safe? So may the Lord reward you with good for what you have done to me this day. ²⁰ And now, behold, I know that you shall surely be king, and that the kingdom of Israel shall be established in your hand. ²¹ Swear to me therefore by the Lord that you will not cut off my offspring after me, and that you will not destroy my name out of my father's house." ²² And David swore this to Saul. Then Saul went home, but David and his men went up to the stronghold.

2 Samuel

1 Then all the tribes of Israel came to David at Hebron and said, "Behold, we are your bone and flesh. *2* In times past, when Saul was king over us, it was you who led out and brought in Israel. And the Lord said to you, 'You shall be shepherd of my people Israel, and you shall be prince over Israel.'" *3* So all the elders of Israel came to the king at Hebron, and King David made a covenant with them at Hebron before the Lord, and they anointed David king over Israel. *4* David was thirty years old when he began to reign, and he reigned forty years. *5* At Hebron he reigned over Judah seven years and six months, and at Jerusalem he reigned over all Israel and Judah thirty-three years.

1 Kings

1 When David's time to die drew near, he commanded Solomon his son, saying, *2* "I am about to go the way of all the earth. Be strong, and show yourself a man, *3* and keep the charge of the Lord your God, walking in his ways and keeping his statutes, his commandments, his rules, and his testimonies, as it is written in the Law of Moses, that you may prosper in all that you do and wherever you turn, *4* that the Lord may establish his word that he spoke concerning me, saying, 'If your sons pay close attention to their way, to walk before me in faithfulness with all their heart and with all their soul, you shall not lack a man on the throne of Israel.'

Acts

16 So Paul stood up, and motioning with his hand said:

"Men of Israel and you who fear God, listen. *17* The God of this people Israel chose our fathers and made the people great during their stay in the land of Egypt, and with uplifted arm he led them out of it. [18] And for about forty years he put up with them in the wilderness. [19] And after destroying seven nations in the land of Canaan, he gave them their land as an inheritance. [20] All this took about 450 years. And after that he gave them judges until Samuel the prophet. [21] Then they asked for a king, and God gave them Saul the son of Kish, a man of the tribe of Benjamin, for forty years. [22] And when he had removed him, he raised up David to be their king, of whom he testified and said, 'I have found in David the son of Jesse a man after my heart, who will do all my will.' [23] Of this man's offspring God has brought to Israel a Savior, Jesus, as he promised.

Discuss: What do these verses teach you about God? What do these verses teach you about your relationship to God?

Third Week of Advent

Hope

Light the first two purple and the pink candles

Return to me, says the Lord of hosts, and I will return to you, says the Lord of hosts.

Zechariah 1:3

Our greatest hope is the promise of reconciliation and right relationship with God, and all the blessings that are part of that relationship.

Suggestions for the week

- Sing *Angels We Have Heard On High*
- Meditate on the hope God has given and still gives to all who are His.
- Thank God for the hope He promises and the many blessings He has already given you.
- Ask yourself how you can bring hope to others in His name.

Pray that God will reveal His truth to you as you read the Scriptures.

Read: Isaiah 11:1-10; Jeremiah 33:14-16

¹ There shall come forth a shoot from the stump of Jesse, and a branch from his roots shall bear fruit.

² And the Spirit of the Lord shall rest upon him, the Spirit of wisdom and understanding, the Spirit of counsel and might, the Spirit of knowledge and the fear of the Lord.

³ And his delight shall be in the fear of the Lord. He shall not judge by what his eyes see, or decide disputes by what his ears hear,

⁴ but with righteousness he shall judge the poor, and decide with equity for the meek of the earth; and he shall strike the earth with the rod of his mouth, and with the breath of his lips he shall kill the wicked.

⁵ Righteousness shall be the belt of his waist, and faithfulness the belt of his loins.

⁶ The wolf shall dwell with the lamb, and the leopard shall lie down with the young goat, and the calf and the lion and the fattened calf together; and a little child shall lead them.

⁷ The cow and the bear shall graze; their young shall lie down together; and the lion shall eat straw like the ox.

⁸ The nursing child shall play over the hole of the cobra, and the weaned child shall put his hand on the adder's den.

⁹ They shall not hurt or destroy in all my holy mountain; for the earth shall be full of the knowledge of the Lord as the waters cover the sea.

¹⁰ In that day the root of Jesse, who shall stand as a signal for the peoples—of him shall the nations inquire, and his resting place shall be glorious.

Jeremiah

¹⁴ "Behold, the days are coming, declares the Lord, when I will fulfill the promise I made to the house of Israel and the house of Judah. ¹⁵ In those days and at that time I will cause a righteous Branch to spring up for David, and he shall execute justice and righteousness in the land. ¹⁶ In those days Judah will be saved, and Jerusalem will dwell securely. And this is the name by which it will be called: 'The Lord is our righteousness.'

Discuss: What do these verses teach you about God? What do these verses teach you about your relationship to God?

Pray that God will reveal His truth to you as you read the Scriptures.

Read: Psalm 110:1-5; 132:11-18; Acts 2:29-36

1 The Lord says to my Lord: "Sit at my right hand, until I make your enemies your footstool."

2 The Lord sends forth from Zion your mighty scepter.   Rule in the midst of your enemies!

3 Your people will offer themselves freely on the day of your power, in holy garments; from the womb of the morning, the dew of your youth will be yours.

4 The Lord has sworn and will not change his mind, "You are a priest forever after the order of Melchizedek."

5 The Lord is at your right hand; he will shatter kings on the day of his wrath.

11 The Lord swore to David a sure oath from which he will not turn back: "One of the sons of your body I will set on your throne.

12 If your sons keep my covenant and my testimonies that I shall teach them, their sons also forever shall sit on your throne."

13 For the Lord has chosen Zion; he has desired it for his dwelling place:

14 "This is my resting place forever; here I will dwell, for I have desired it.

15 I will abundantly bless her provisions; I will satisfy her poor with bread.

16 Her priests I will clothe with salvation, and her saints will shout for joy.

¹⁷ There I will make a horn to sprout for David; I have prepared a lamp for my anointed.

¹⁸ His enemies I will clothe with shame, but on him his crown will shine."

Acts

²⁹ "Brothers, I may say to you with confidence about the patriarch David that he both died and was buried, and his tomb is with us to this day. ³⁰ Being therefore a prophet, and knowing that God had sworn with an oath to him that he would set one of his descendants on his throne, ³¹ he foresaw and spoke about the resurrection of the Christ, that he was not abandoned to Hades, nor did his flesh see corruption. ³² This Jesus God raised up, and of that we all are witnesses. ³³ Being therefore exalted at the right hand of God, and having received from the Father the promise of the Holy Spirit, he has poured out this that you yourselves are seeing and hearing. ³⁴ For David did not ascend into the heavens, but he himself says,

"'The Lord said to my Lord, "Sit at my right hand,

³⁵ until I make your enemies your footstool."'

³⁶ Let all the house of Israel therefore know for certain that God has made him both Lord and Christ, this Jesus whom you crucified."

Discuss: What do these verses teach you about God? What do these verses teach you about your relationship to God?

Third Tuesday of Advent

Pray that God will reveal His truth to you as you read the Scriptures.

Read: Isaiah 53:1-12

> [1] Who has believed what he has heard from us?
>> And to whom has the arm of the Lord been revealed?
> [2] For he grew up before him like a young plant,
>> and like a root out of dry ground;
> he had no form or majesty that we should look at him,
>> and no beauty that we should desire him.
> [3] He was despised and rejected by men;
>> a man of sorrows, and acquainted with grief;
> and as one from whom men hide their faces
>> he was despised, and we esteemed him not.
> [4] Surely he has borne our griefs
>> and carried our sorrows;
> yet we esteemed him stricken,
>> smitten by God, and afflicted.
> [5] But he was pierced for our transgressions;
>> he was crushed for our iniquities;
> upon him was the chastisement that brought us peace,
>> and with his wounds we are healed.
> [6] All we like sheep have gone astray;
>> we have turned—every one—to his own way;
> and the Lord has laid on him
>> the iniquity of us all.
> [7] He was oppressed, and he was afflicted,

yet he opened not his mouth;
like a lamb that is led to the slaughter,
    and like a sheep that before its shearers is silent,
    so he opened not his mouth.
8 By oppression and judgment he was taken away;
    and as for his generation, who considered
that he was cut off out of the land of the living,
    stricken for the transgression of my people?
9 And they made his grave with the wicked
    and with a rich man in his death,
although he had done no violence,
    and there was no deceit in his mouth.
10 Yet it was the will of the Lord to crush him;
    he has put him to grief;
when his soul makes an offering for guilt,
    he shall see his offspring; he shall prolong his days;
the will of the Lord shall prosper in his hand.
11 Out of the anguish of his soul he shall see and be satisfied;
by his knowledge shall the righteous one, my servant,
    make many to be accounted righteous,
    and he shall bear their iniquities.
12 Therefore I will divide him a portion with the many,
    and he shall divide the spoil with the strong,
because he poured out his soul to death
    and was numbered with the transgressors;
yet he bore the sin of many,
    and makes intercession for the transgressors.

Discuss: What do these verses teach you about God? What do these verses teach you about your relationship to God?

Pray that God will reveal His truth to you as you read the Scriptures.

Read: Isaiah 60:1-6, 10-12, 14-16, 18-22

> [1] Arise, shine, for your light has come,
>> and the glory of the Lord has risen upon you.
> [2] For behold, darkness shall cover the earth,
>> and thick darkness the peoples;
> but the Lord will arise upon you,
>> and his glory will be seen upon you.
> [3] And nations shall come to your light,
>> and kings to the brightness of your rising.
> [4] Lift up your eyes all around, and see;
>> they all gather together, they come to you;
> your sons shall come from afar,
>> and your daughters shall be carried on the hip.
> [5] Then you shall see and be radiant;
>> your heart shall thrill and exult,
> because the abundance of the sea shall be turned to you,
>> the wealth of the nations shall come to you.
> [6] A multitude of camels shall cover you,
>> the young camels of Midian and Ephah;
>> all those from Sheba shall come.
> They shall bring gold and frankincense,
>> and shall bring good news, the praises of the Lord.

> [10] Foreigners shall build up your walls,

and their kings shall minister to you;
for in my wrath I struck you,
    but in my favor I have had mercy on you.
[11] Your gates shall be open continually;
    day and night they shall not be shut,
that people may bring to you the wealth of the nations,
    with their kings led in procession.
[12] For the nation and kingdom
    that will not serve you shall perish;
    those nations shall be utterly laid waste.

[14] The sons of those who afflicted you
    shall come bending low to you,
and all who despised you
    shall bow down at your feet;
they shall call you the City of the Lord,
    the Zion of the Holy One of Israel.
[15] Whereas you have been forsaken and hated,
    with no one passing through,
I will make you majestic forever,
    a joy from age to age.
[16] You shall suck the milk of nations;
    you shall nurse at the breast of kings;
and you shall know that I, the Lord, am your Savior
    and your Redeemer, the Mighty One of Jacob.

[18] Violence shall no more be heard in your land,
    devastation or destruction within your borders;
you shall call your walls Salvation,

and your gates Praise.

¹⁹ The sun shall be no more
    your light by day,
nor for brightness shall the moon
    give you light;
but the Lord will be your everlasting light,
    and your God will be your glory.
²⁰ Your sun shall no more go down,
    nor your moon withdraw itself;
for the Lord will be your everlasting light,
    and your days of mourning shall be ended.
²¹ Your people shall all be righteous;
    they shall possess the land forever,
the branch of my planting, the work of my hands,
    that I might be glorified.
²² The least one shall become a clan,
    and the smallest one a mighty nation;
I am the Lord;
    in its time I will hasten it.

Discuss: What do these verses teach you about God? What do these verses teach you about your relationship to God?

Pray that God will reveal His truth to you as you read the Scriptures.

Read: Zechariah 3:3-9, 12:10-11, 13:1

3 Now Joshua was standing before the angel, clothed with filthy garments. *4* And the angel said to those who were standing before him, "Remove the filthy garments from him." And to him he said, "Behold, I have taken your iniquity away from you, and I will clothe you with pure vestments." *5* And I said, "Let them put a clean turban on his head." So they put a clean turban on his head and clothed him with garments. And the angel of the Lord was standing by.

6 And the angel of the Lord solemnly assured Joshua, *7* "Thus says the Lord of hosts: If you will walk in my ways and keep my charge, then you shall rule my house and have charge of my courts, and I will give you the right of access among those who are standing here. *8* Hear now, O Joshua the high priest, you and your friends who sit before you, for they are men who are a sign: behold, I will bring my servant the Branch. *9* For behold, on the stone that I have set before Joshua, on a single stone with seven eyes, I will engrave its inscription, declares the Lord of hosts, and I will remove the iniquity of this land in a single day.

10 "And I will pour out on the house of David and the inhabitants of Jerusalem a spirit of grace and pleas for mercy, so that, when they look on me, on him whom they have pierced, they shall mourn for him, as one mourns for an only child, and weep bitterly over him, as one weeps over a firstborn. *11* On that day the mourning in Jerusalem will be as great as the mourning for Hadad-rimmon in the plain of Megiddo.

1 "On that day there shall be a fountain opened for the house of David and the inhabitants of Jerusalem, to cleanse them from sin and uncleanness.

Discuss: What do these verses teach you about God? What do these verses teach you about your relationship to God?

Third Friday of Advent

Pray that God will reveal His truth to you as you read the Scriptures.

Read: Isaiah 52:7-10; 40:9-11; 43:1; 62:11-12; Malachi 3:1; Zechariah 9:9

> *7* How beautiful upon the mountains
>   are the feet of him who brings good news,
> who publishes peace, who brings good news of happiness,
>   who publishes salvation,
>   who says to Zion, "Your God reigns."
> *8* The voice of your watchmen—they lift up their voice;
>   together they sing for joy;
> for eye to eye they see
>   the return of the Lord to Zion.
> *9* Break forth together into singing,
>   you waste places of Jerusalem,
> for the Lord has comforted his people;
>   he has redeemed Jerusalem.
> *10* The Lord has bared his holy arm
>   before the eyes of all the nations,
> and all the ends of the earth shall see
>   the salvation of our God.

> *9* Go on up to a high mountain,
>   O Zion, herald of good news;
> lift up your voice with strength,
>   O Jerusalem, herald of good news;
>   lift it up, fear not;

say to the cities of Judah,
   "Behold your God!"
[10] Behold, the Lord God comes with might,
   and his arm rules for him;
behold, his reward is with him,
   and his recompense before him.
[11] He will tend his flock like a shepherd;
   he will gather the lambs in his arms;
he will carry them in his bosom,
   and gently lead those that are with young.

[1] But now thus says the Lord,
he who created you, O Jacob,
   he who formed you, O Israel:
"Fear not, for I have redeemed you;
   I have called you by name, you are mine.

[11] Behold, the Lord has proclaimed
   to the end of the earth:
Say to the daughter of Zion,
   "Behold, your salvation comes;
behold, his reward is with him,
   and his recompense before him."
[12] And they shall be called The Holy People,
   The Redeemed of the Lord;
and you shall be called Sought Out,
   A City Not Forsaken.

Malachi

¹ "Behold, I send my messenger, and he will prepare the way before me. And the Lord whom you seek will suddenly come to his temple; and the messenger of the covenant in whom you delight, behold, he is coming, says the Lord of hosts.

Zechariah

⁹ Rejoice greatly, O daughter of Zion!
   Shout aloud, O daughter of Jerusalem!
Behold, your king is coming to you;
   righteous and having salvation is he,
humble and mounted on a donkey,
   on a colt, the foal of a donkey.

Discuss: What do these verses teach you about God? What do these verses teach you about your relationship to God?

Pray that God will reveal His truth to you as you read the Scriptures.

Read: Isaiah 40:1-3, 5; Luke 1:5-25; Matthew 3:3

> [1] Comfort, comfort my people, says your God.
>
> [2] Speak tenderly to Jerusalem,
>> and cry to her
>
> that her warfare is ended,
>> that her iniquity is pardoned,
>
> that she has received from the Lord's hand
>> double for all her sins.
>
> [3] A voice cries:
>
> "In the wilderness prepare the way of the Lord;
>> make straight in the desert a highway for our God.
>
> [5] And the glory of the Lord shall be revealed,
>> and all flesh shall see it together,
>> for the mouth of the Lord has spoken."

Luke

[5] In the days of Herod, king of Judea, there was a priest named Zechariah, of the division of Abijah. And he had a wife from the daughters of Aaron, and her name was Elizabeth. [6] And they were both righteous before God, walking blamelessly in all the commandments and statutes of the Lord. [7] But they had no child, because Elizabeth was barren, and both were advanced in years.

⁸ Now while he was serving as priest before God when his division was on duty, ⁹ according to the custom of the priesthood, he was chosen by lot to enter the temple of the Lord and burn incense. ¹⁰ And the whole multitude of the people were praying outside at the hour of incense. ¹¹ And there appeared to him an angel of the Lord standing on the right side of the altar of incense. ¹² And Zechariah was troubled when he saw him, and fear fell upon him. ¹³ But the angel said to him, "Do not be afraid, Zechariah, for your prayer has been heard, and your wife Elizabeth will bear you a son, and you shall call his name John. ¹⁴ And you will have joy and gladness, and many will rejoice at his birth, ¹⁵ for he will be great before the Lord. And he must not drink wine or strong drink, and he will be filled with the Holy Spirit, even from his mother's womb. ¹⁶ And he will turn many of the children of Israel to the Lord their God, ¹⁷ and he will go before him in the spirit and power of Elijah, to turn the hearts of the fathers to the children, and the disobedient to the wisdom of the just, to make ready for the Lord a people prepared."

¹⁸ And Zechariah said to the angel, "How shall I know this? For I am an old man, and my wife is advanced in years." ¹⁹ And the angel answered him, "I am Gabriel. I stand in the presence of God, and I was sent to speak to you and to bring you this good news. ²⁰ And behold, you will be silent and unable to speak until the day that these things take place, because you did not believe my words, which will be fulfilled in their time." ²¹ And the people were waiting for Zechariah, and they were wondering at his delay in the temple. ²² And when he came out, he was unable to speak to them, and they realized that he had seen a vision in the tem-

ple. And he kept making signs to them and remained mute. [23] And when his time of service was ended, he went to his home.

[24] After these days his wife Elizabeth conceived, and for five months she kept herself hidden, saying, [25] "Thus the Lord has done for me in the days when he looked on me, to take away my reproach among people."

Matthew

[3] For this is he who was spoken of by the prophet Isaiah when he said,

"The voice of one crying in the wilderness:

'Prepare the way of the Lord;

make his paths straight.'"

Discuss: What do these verses teach you about God? What do these verses teach you about your relationship to God?

Peace
Light all the colored candles

My eyes long for your salvation and for the fulfillment of your righteous promise.

Psalm 119:123

Blessed is the King who comes in the name of the Lord! Peace in heaven and glory in the highest!

Luke 19:38

Jesus is the fulfillment of the promise of reconciliation and peace with God. Meditate on these awesome attributes of Jesus.

Suggestions for the week

- Sing *O Come All Ye Faithful*
- As you read the passages about Jesus this week, make note of details about Him you had forgotten or had previously not known.
- Spend time praising and thanking Him for the gift of salvation.
- Consider whether there is an area of your life in which you are not at peace and what you should do about it.

Fourth Sunday of Advent

Pray that God will reveal His truth to you as you read the Scriptures.

Read: Luke 1:26-80,2:1-20; Matthew 1:18-25

26 In the sixth month the angel Gabriel was sent from God to a city of Galilee named Nazareth, 27 to a virgin betrothed to a man whose name was Joseph, of the house of David. And the virgin's name was Mary. 28 And he came to her and said, "Greetings, O favored one, the Lord is with you!" 29 But she was greatly troubled at the saying, and tried to discern what sort of greeting this might be. 30 And the angel said to her, "Do not be afraid, Mary, for you have found favor with God. 31 And behold, you will conceive in your womb and bear a son, and you shall call his name Jesus. 32 He will be great and will be called the Son of the Most High. And the Lord God will give to him the throne of his father David, 33 and he will reign over the house of Jacob forever, and of his kingdom there will be no end."

34 And Mary said to the angel, "How will this be, since I am a virgin?"

35 And the angel answered her, "The Holy Spirit will come upon you, and the power of the Most High will overshadow you; therefore the child to be born will be called holy—the Son of God. 36 And behold, your relative Elizabeth in her old age has also conceived a son, and this is the sixth month with her who was called barren. 37 For nothing will be impossible with God." 38 And Mary said, "Behold, I am the servant of the Lord; let it be to me according to your word." And the angel departed from her.

Matthew

[18] Now the birth of Jesus Christ took place in this way. When his mother Mary had been betrothed to Joseph, before they came together she was found to be with child from the Holy Spirit. [19] And her husband Joseph, being a just man and unwilling to put her to shame, resolved to divorce her quietly. [20] But as he considered these things, behold, an angel of the Lord appeared to him in a dream, saying, "Joseph, son of David, do not fear to take Mary as your wife, for that which is conceived in her is from the Holy Spirit. [21] She will bear a son, and you shall call his name Jesus, for he will save his people from their sins." [22] All this took place to fulfill what the Lord had spoken by the prophet:

[23] "Behold, the virgin shall conceive and bear a son, and they shall call his name Immanuel" (which means, God with us).

[24] When Joseph woke from sleep, he did as the angel of the Lord commanded him: he took his wife, [25] but knew her not until she had given birth to a son. And he called his name Jesus.

Luke

[39] In those days Mary arose and went with haste into the hill country, to a town in Judah, [40] and she entered the house of Zechariah and greeted Elizabeth. [41] And when Elizabeth heard the greeting of Mary, the baby leaped in her womb. And Elizabeth was filled with the Holy Spirit, [42] and she exclaimed with a loud cry, "Blessed are you among women, and blessed is the fruit of your womb! [43] And why is this granted to me that the mother of my Lord should come to me? [44] For behold, when the sound of your greeting came to my ears, the baby in my womb leaped for joy. [45] And blessed is she who believed that there would be a fulfillment of what was spoken to her from the Lord."

⁴⁶ And Mary said, "My soul magnifies the Lord,

⁴⁷ and my spirit rejoices in God my Savior,

⁴⁸ for he has looked on the humble estate of his servant. For behold, from now on all generations will call me blessed;

⁴⁹ for he who is mighty has done great things for me, and holy is his name.

⁵⁰ And his mercy is for those who fear him from generation to generation.

⁵¹ He has shown strength with his arm;

he has scattered the proud in the thoughts of their hearts;

⁵² he has brought down the mighty from their thrones

and exalted those of humble estate;

⁵³ he has filled the hungry with good things,

and the rich he has sent away empty.

⁵⁴ He has helped his servant Israel,

in remembrance of his mercy,

⁵⁵ as he spoke to our fathers,

to Abraham and to his offspring forever."

⁵⁶ And Mary remained with her about three months and returned to her home.

⁵⁷ Now the time came for Elizabeth to give birth, and she bore a son. ⁵⁸ And her neighbors and relatives heard that the Lord had shown great mercy to her, and they rejoiced with her. ⁵⁹ And on the eighth day they came to circumcise the child. And they would have called him Zechariah after his father, ⁶⁰ but his mother answered, "No; he shall be called John." ⁶¹ And they said to her, "None of your relatives is called by this name." ⁶² And they made signs to his father, inquiring what he wanted him to be called. ⁶³ And he asked for a writing tablet and wrote, "His name is John."

And they all wondered. [64] And immediately his mouth was opened and his tongue loosed, and he spoke, blessing God. [65] And fear came on all their neighbors. And all these things were talked about through all the hill country of Judea, [66] and all who heard them laid them up in their hearts, saying, "What then will this child be?" For the hand of the Lord was with him.

[67] And his father Zechariah was filled with the Holy Spirit and prophesied, saying,

[68] "Blessed be the Lord God of Israel, for he has visited and redeemed his people

[69] and has raised up a horn of salvation for us in the house of his servant David,

[70] as he spoke by the mouth of his holy prophets from of old,

[71] that we should be saved from our enemies and from the hand of all who hate us;

[72] to show the mercy promised to our fathers and to remember his holy covenant,

[73] the oath that he swore to our father Abraham, to grant us

[74] that we, being delivered from the hand of our enemies, might serve him without fear,

[75] in holiness and righteousness before him all our days.

[76] And you, child, will be called the prophet of the Most High; for you will go before the Lord to prepare his ways,

[77] to give knowledge of salvation to his people in the forgiveness of their sins,

[78] because of the tender mercy of our God, whereby the sunrise shall visit us from on high

[79] to give light to those who sit in darkness and in the shadow of death, to guide our feet into the way of peace."

⁸⁰ And the child grew and became strong in spirit, and he was in the wilderness until the day of his public appearance to Israel.

Luke

¹ In those days a decree went out from Caesar Augustus that all the world should be registered. ² This was the first registration when Quirinius was governor of Syria. ³ And all went to be registered, each to his own town. ⁴ And Joseph also went up from Galilee, from the town of Nazareth, to Judea, to the city of David, which is called Bethlehem, because he was of the house and lineage of David, ⁵ to be registered with Mary, his betrothed, who was with child. ⁶ And while they were there, the time came for her to give birth. ⁷ And she gave birth to her firstborn son and wrapped him in swaddling cloths and laid him in a manger, because there was no place for them in the inn.

⁸ And in the same region there were shepherds out in the field, keeping watch over their flock by night. ⁹ And an angel of the Lord appeared to them, and the glory of the Lord shone around them, and they were filled with great fear. ¹⁰ And the angel said to them, "Fear not, for behold, I bring you good news of great joy that will be for all the people. ¹¹ For unto you is born this day in the city of David a Savior, who is Christ the Lord. ¹² And this will be a sign for you: you will find a baby wrapped in swaddling cloths and lying in a manger." ¹³ And suddenly there was with the angel a multitude of the heavenly host praising God and saying,

¹⁴ "Glory to God in the highest, and on earth peace among those with whom he is pleased!"

¹⁵ When the angels went away from them into heaven, the shepherds said to one another, "Let us go over to Bethlehem and

see this thing that has happened, which the Lord has made known to us." [16] And they went with haste and found Mary and Joseph, and the baby lying in a manger. [17] And when they saw it, they made known the saying that had been told them concerning this child. [18] And all who heard it wondered at what the shepherds told them. [19] But Mary treasured up all these things, pondering them in her heart. [20] And the shepherds returned, glorifying and praising God for all they had heard and seen, as it had been told them.

Discuss: What do these verses teach you about God? What do these verses teach you about your relationship to God?

Pray that God will reveal His truth to you as you read the Scriptures.

Read: Luke 2:21-38; 41-52; Matthew 2:1-23

[21] And at the end of eight days, when he was circumcised, he was called Jesus, the name given by the angel before he was conceived in the womb. [22] And when the time came for their purification according to the Law of Moses, they brought him up to Jerusalem to present him to the Lord [23] (as it is written in the Law of the Lord, "Every male who first opens the womb shall be called holy to the Lord") [24] and to offer a sacrifice according to what is said in the Law of the Lord, "a pair of turtledoves, or two young pigeons." [25] Now there was a man in Jerusalem, whose name was Simeon, and this man was righteous and devout, waiting for the consolation of Israel, and the Holy Spirit was upon him. [26] And it had been revealed to him by the Holy Spirit that he would not see death before he had seen the Lord's Christ. [27] And he came in the Spirit into the temple, and when the parents brought in the child Jesus, to do for him according to the custom of the Law, [28] he took him up in his arms and blessed God and said,

[29] "Lord, now you are letting your servant depart in peace, according to your word;

[30] for my eyes have seen your salvation

[31] that you have prepared in the presence of all peoples,

[32] a light for revelation to the Gentiles, and for glory to your people Israel."

33 And his father and his mother marveled at what was said about him. *34* And Simeon blessed them and said to Mary his mother, "Behold, this child is appointed for the fall and rising of many in Israel, and for a sign that is opposed *35* (and a sword will pierce through your own soul also), so that thoughts from many hearts may be revealed."

36 And there was a prophetess, Anna, the daughter of Phanuel, of the tribe of Asher. She was advanced in years, having lived with her husband seven years from when she was a virgin, *37* and then as a widow until she was eighty-four. She did not depart from the temple, worshiping with fasting and prayer night and day. *38* And coming up at that very hour she began to give thanks to God and to speak of him to all who were waiting for the redemption of Jerusalem.

Matthew

1 Now after Jesus was born in Bethlehem of Judea in the days of Herod the king, behold, wise men from the east came to Jerusalem, *2* saying, "Where is he who has been born king of the Jews? For we saw his star when it rose and have come to worship him." *3* When Herod the king heard this, he was troubled, and all Jerusalem with him; *4* and assembling all the chief priests and scribes of the people, he inquired of them where the Christ was to be born. *5* They told him, "In Bethlehem of Judea, for so it is written by the prophet:

6 "'And you, O Bethlehem, in the land of Judah, are by no means least among the rulers of Judah; for from you shall come a ruler who will shepherd my people Israel.'"

⁷ Then Herod summoned the wise men secretly and ascertained from them what time the star had appeared. ⁸ And he sent them to Bethlehem, saying, "Go and search diligently for the child, and when you have found him, bring me word, that I too may come and worship him." ⁹ After listening to the king, they went on their way. And behold, the star that they had seen when it rose went before them until it came to rest over the place where the child was. ¹⁰ When they saw the star, they rejoiced exceedingly with great joy. ¹¹ And going into the house they saw the child with Mary his mother, and they fell down and worshiped him. Then, opening their treasures, they offered him gifts, gold and frankincense and myrrh. ¹² And being warned in a dream not to return to Herod, they departed to their own country by another way.

¹³ Now when they had departed, behold, an angel of the Lord appeared to Joseph in a dream and said, "Rise, take the child and his mother, and flee to Egypt, and remain there until I tell you, for Herod is about to search for the child, to destroy him." ¹⁴ And he rose and took the child and his mother by night and departed to Egypt ¹⁵ and remained there until the death of Herod. This was to fulfill what the Lord had spoken by the prophet, "Out of Egypt I called my son."

¹⁶ Then Herod, when he saw that he had been tricked by the wise men, became furious, and he sent and killed all the male children in Bethlehem and in all that region who were two years old or under, according to the time that he had ascertained from the wise men. ¹⁷ Then was fulfilled what was spoken by the prophet Jeremiah:

¹⁸ "A voice was heard in Ramah, weeping and loud lamentation, Rachel weeping for her children; she refused to be comforted, because they are no more."

¹⁹ But when Herod died, behold, an angel of the Lord appeared in a dream to Joseph in Egypt, ²⁰ saying, "Rise, take the child and his mother and go to the land of Israel, for those who sought the child's life are dead." ²¹ And he rose and took the child and his mother and went to the land of Israel. ²² But when he heard that Archelaus was reigning over Judea in place of his father Herod, he was afraid to go there, and being warned in a dream he withdrew to the district of Galilee. ²³ And he went and lived in a city called Nazareth, so that what was spoken by the prophets might be fulfilled, that he would be called a Nazarene.

Luke

⁴¹ Now his parents went to Jerusalem every year at the Feast of the Passover. ⁴² And when he was twelve years old, they went up according to custom. ⁴³ And when the feast was ended, as they were returning, the boy Jesus stayed behind in Jerusalem. His parents did not know it, ⁴⁴ but supposing him to be in the group they went a day's journey, but then they began to search for him among their relatives and acquaintances, ⁴⁵ and when they did not find him, they returned to Jerusalem, searching for him. ⁴⁶ After three days they found him in the temple, sitting among the teachers, listening to them and asking them questions. ⁴⁷ And all who heard him were amazed at his understanding and his answers. ⁴⁸ And when his parents saw him, they were astonished. And his mother said to him, "Son, why have you treated us so? Behold, your father and I have been searching for you in great distress." ⁴⁹ And he said to them, "Why were you looking for me?

Did you not know that I must be in my Father's house?" *50* And they did not understand the saying that he spoke to them. *51* And he went down with them and came to Nazareth and was submissive to them. And his mother treasured up all these things in her heart.

52 And Jesus increased in wisdom and in stature and in favor with God and man.

Discuss: What do these verses teach you about God? What do these verses teach you about your relationship to God?

Fourth Tuesday of Advent

Pray that God will reveal His truth to you as you read the Scriptures.

Read: John 13:1; 17:1-5; Luke 22:39; Matthew 26:47; John 18:12; Luke 23:1,3,13-16,21,24,34-38,44-47,52-56; Mark 16:1-6, 9, 12, 14-16; Acts 1:6-11

John

¹ Now before the Feast of the Passover, when Jesus knew that his hour had come to depart out of this world to the Father, having loved his own who were in the world, he loved them to the end.

¹ When Jesus had spoken these words, he lifted up his eyes to heaven, and said, "Father, the hour has come; glorify your Son that the Son may glorify you, ² since you have given him authority over all flesh, to give eternal life to all whom you have given him. ³ And this is eternal life, that they know you the only true God, and Jesus Christ whom you have sent. ⁴ I glorified you on earth, having accomplished the work that you gave me to do. ⁵ And now, Father, glorify me in your own presence with the glory that I had with you before the world existed.

Luke

³⁹ And he came out and went, as was his custom, to the Mount of Olives, and the disciples followed him.

Matthew

⁴⁷ While he was still speaking, Judas came, one of the twelve, and with him a great crowd with swords and clubs, from the chief priests and the elders of the people.

John

¹² So the band of soldiers and their captain and the officers of the Jews arrested Jesus and bound him.

Luke

¹ Then the whole company of them arose and brought him before Pilate. ³ And Pilate asked him, "Are you the King of the Jews?" And he answered him, "You have said so."

¹³ Pilate then called together the chief priests and the rulers and the people, ¹⁴ and said to them, "You brought me this man as one who was misleading the people. And after examining him before you, behold, I did not find this man guilty of any of your charges against him. ¹⁵ Neither did Herod, for he sent him back to us. Look, nothing deserving death has been done by him. ¹⁶ I will therefore punish and release him."

²¹ but they kept shouting, "Crucify, crucify him!"²⁴ So Pilate decided that their demand should be granted.

³⁴ And Jesus said, "Father, forgive them, for they know not what they do." And they cast lots to divide his garments. ³⁵ And the people stood by, watching, but the rulers scoffed at him, saying, "He saved others; let him save himself, if he is the Christ of God, his Chosen One!" ³⁶ The soldiers also mocked him, coming up and offering him sour wine ³⁷ and saying, "If you are the King of the Jews, save yourself!" ³⁸ There was also an inscription over him, "This is the King of the Jews."

⁴⁴ It was now about the sixth hour, and there was darkness over the whole land until the ninth hour, ⁴⁵ while the sun's light failed. And the curtain of the temple was torn in two. ⁴⁶ Then Je-

sus, calling out with a loud voice, said, "Father, into your hands I commit my spirit!" And having said this he breathed his last. [47] Now when the centurion saw what had taken place, he praised God, saying, "Certainly this man was innocent!"[52] This man went to Pilate and asked for the body of Jesus. [53] Then he took it down and wrapped it in a linen shroud and laid him in a tomb cut in stone, where no one had ever yet been laid. [54] It was the day of Preparation, and the Sabbath was beginning. [55] The women who had come with him from Galilee followed and saw the tomb and how his body was laid. [56] Then they returned and prepared spices and ointments. On the Sabbath they rested according to the commandment.

Mark

[1] When the Sabbath was past, Mary Magdalene, Mary the mother of James, and Salome bought spices, so that they might go and anoint him. [2] And very early on the first day of the week, when the sun had risen, they went to the tomb. [3] And they were saying to one another, "Who will roll away the stone for us from the entrance of the tomb?" [4] And looking up, they saw that the stone had been rolled back—it was very large. [5] And entering the tomb, they saw a young man sitting on the right side, dressed in a white robe, and they were alarmed. [6] And he said to them, "Do not be alarmed. You seek Jesus of Nazareth, who was crucified. He has risen; he is not here. See the place where they laid him.

[9] Now when he rose early on the first day of the week, he appeared first to Mary Magdalene, from whom he had cast out seven demons.

[12] After these things he appeared in another form to two of them, as they were walking into the country.

14 Afterward he appeared to the eleven themselves as they were reclining at table, and he rebuked them for their unbelief and hardness of heart, because they had not believed those who saw him after he had risen. *15* And he said to them, "Go into all the world and proclaim the gospel to the whole creation. *16* Whoever believes and is baptized will be saved, but whoever does not believe will be condemned.

Acts

6 So when they had come together, they asked him, "Lord, will you at this time restore the kingdom to Israel?" *7* He said to them, "It is not for you to know times or seasons that the Father has fixed by his own authority. *8* But you will receive power when the Holy Spirit has come upon you, and you will be my witnesses in Jerusalem and in all Judea and Samaria, and to the end of the earth." *9* And when he had said these things, as they were looking on, he was lifted up, and a cloud took him out of their sight. *10* And while they were gazing into heaven as he went, behold, two men stood by them in white robes, *11* and said, "Men of Galilee, why do you stand looking into heaven? This Jesus, who was taken up from you into heaven, will come in the same way as you saw him go into heaven."

Discuss: What do these verses teach you about God?   What do these verses teach you about your relationship to God?

Love
Light all the colored candles and the white candle

*For God so loved the world, that he gave his only Son, that who-
ever believes in him should not perish but have eternal life.*

John 3:16

A person may give his or her most prized possession to the person he or she most loves; we may appreciate receiving that which
we know the giver has highly valued. But, God gave more than
any human could ever give or expect to receive: His perfect, sin-
less Son to die that we might live.

Suggestions for the week

- Sing *Hark the Herald Angels Sing*
- Meditate on the greatness of a God who would purpose that
  His Son would humble himself to be born and to live among us
  and to die to provide a means of reconciliation for us sinners.
- Ask yourself how you can demonstrate God's sacrificial love for
  you by sacrificially loving someone in the coming year in His
  name.

Christmas Day

Pray that God will reveal His truth to you as you read the Scriptures.

Read: Revelation 1:1-4; 4:1; 7:9-12; 21:1-6, 22-27; 22:3-21

1 The revelation of Jesus Christ, which God gave him to show to his servants the things that must soon take place. He made it known by sending his angel to his servant John, *2* who bore witness to the word of God and to the testimony of Jesus Christ, even to all that he saw. *3* Blessed is the one who reads aloud the words of this prophecy, and blessed are those who hear, and who keep what is written in it, for the time is near.

4 John to the seven churches that are in Asia:

Grace to you and peace from him who is and who was and who is to come, and from the seven spirits who are before his throne,

1 After this I looked, and behold, a door standing open in heaven! And the first voice, which I had heard speaking to me like a trumpet, said, "Come up here, and I will show you what must take place after this."

9 After this I looked, and behold, a great multitude that no one could number, from every nation, from all tribes and peoples and languages, standing before the throne and before the Lamb, clothed in white robes, with palm branches in their hands, *10* and crying out with a loud voice, "Salvation belongs to our God who sits on the throne, and to the Lamb!" *11* And all the angels were standing around the throne and around the elders and the four living creatures, and they fell on their faces before the throne and worshiped God, *12* saying, "Amen! Blessing and glory and wisdom and thanksgiving and honor and power and might be to our God forever and ever! Amen."

1 Then I saw a new heaven and a new earth, for the first heaven and the first earth had passed away, and the sea was no more. *2* And I saw the holy city, new Jerusalem, coming down out of heaven from God, prepared as a bride adorned for her husband. *3* And I heard a loud voice from the throne saying, "Behold, the dwelling place of God is with man. He will dwell with them, and they will be his people, and God himself will be with them as their God. *4* He will wipe away every tear from their eyes, and death shall be no more, neither shall there be mourning, nor crying, nor pain anymore, for the former things have passed away."

5 And he who was seated on the throne said, "Behold, I am making all things new." Also he said, "Write this down, for these words are trustworthy and true." *6* And he said to me, "It is done! I am the Alpha and the Omega, the beginning and the end. To the thirsty I will give from the spring of the water of life without payment.

22 And I saw no temple in the city, for its temple is the Lord God the Almighty and the Lamb. *23* And the city has no need of sun or moon to shine on it, for the glory of God gives it light, and its lamp is the Lamb. *24* By its light will the nations walk, and the kings of the earth will bring their glory into it, *25* and its gates will never be shut by day—and there will be no night there. *26* They will bring into it the glory and the honor of the nations. *27* But nothing unclean will ever enter it, nor anyone who does what is detestable or false, but only those who are written in the Lamb's book of life.

3 No longer will there be anything accursed, but the throne of God and of the Lamb will be in it, and his servants will worship him. *4* They will see his face, and his name will be on their foreheads. *5* And night will be no more. They will need no light of lamp or sun, for the Lord God will be their light, and they will reign forever and ever.

6 And he said to me, "These words are trustworthy and true. And the Lord, the God of the spirits of the prophets, has sent his angel to show his servants what must soon take place."

7 "And behold, I am coming soon. Blessed is the one who keeps the words of the prophecy of this book."

8 I, John, am the one who heard and saw these things. And when I heard and saw them, I fell down to worship at the feet of the angel who showed them to me, *9* but he said to me, "You must not do that! I am a fellow servant with you and your brothers the prophets, and with those who keep the words of this book. Worship God."

10 And he said to me, "Do not seal up the words of the prophecy of this book, for the time is near. *11* Let the evildoer still do evil, and the filthy still be filthy, and the righteous still do right, and the holy still be holy."

12 "Behold, I am coming soon, bringing my recompense with me, to repay each one for what he has done. *13* I am the Alpha and the Omega, the first and the last, the beginning and the end."

¹⁴ Blessed are those who wash their robes, so that they may have the right to the tree of life and that they may enter the city by the gates. ¹⁵ Outside are the dogs and sorcerers and the sexually immoral and murderers and idolaters, and everyone who loves and practices falsehood.

¹⁶ "I, Jesus, have sent my angel to testify to you about these things for the churches. I am the root and the descendant of David, the bright morning star."

¹⁷ The Spirit and the Bride say, "Come." And let the one who hears say, "Come." And let the one who is thirsty come; let the one who desires take the water of life without price.

¹⁸ I warn everyone who hears the words of the prophecy of this book: if anyone adds to them, God will add to him the plagues described in this book, ¹⁹ and if anyone takes away from the words of the book of this prophecy, God will take away his share in the tree of life and in the holy city, which are described in this book.

²⁰ He who testifies to these things says, "Surely I am coming soon." Amen. Come, Lord Jesus!

²¹ The grace of the Lord Jesus be with all. Amen.

Songs

O Come O Come Emmanuel

Joy to the World

Angels We Have Heard On High

O Come All Ye Faithful

Hark the Herald Angels Sing

O Come O Come Emmanuel

O come, O come, Emmanuel
And ransom captive Israel
That mourns in lonely exile here
Until the Son of God appear

Refrain
Rejoice! Rejoice! Emmanuel
Shall come to thee, O Israel.

O come, Thou Rod of Jesse, free
Thine own from Satan's tyranny
From depths of Hell Thy people save
And give them victory o'er the grave

Refrain

O come, Thou Day-Spring, come and cheer
Our spirits by Thine advent here
Disperse the gloomy clouds of night
And death's dark shadows put to flight.

Refrain

O come, Thou Key of David, come,
And open wide our heavenly home;
Make safe the way that leads on high,
And close the path to misery.

Refrain

O come, O come, Thou Lord of might,
Who to Thy tribes, on Sinai's height,
In ancient times did'st give the Law,
In cloud, and majesty and awe.

Refrain

Joy to the World

Joy to the World, the Lord is come!
Let earth receive her King;
Let every heart prepare Him room,
And Heaven and nature sing,
And Heaven and nature sing,
And Heaven, and Heaven, and nature sing.

Joy to the World, the Savior reigns!
Let men their songs employ;
While fields and floods, rocks, hills and plains
Repeat the sounding joy,
Repeat the sounding joy,
Repeat, repeat, the sounding joy.

No more let sins and sorrows grow,
Nor thorns infest the ground;
He comes to make His blessings flow
Far as the curse is found,
Far as the curse is found,
Far as, far as, the curse is found.

He rules the world with truth and grace,
And makes the nations prove
The glories of His righteousness,
And wonders of His love,
And wonders of His love,
And wonders, wonders, of His love.

Angels We Have Heard On High

Angels we have heard on high
Sweetly singing o'er the plains,
And the mountains in reply
Echoing their joyous strains.

Refrain
Gloria, in excelsis Deo!
Gloria, in excelsis Deo!

Shepherds, why this jubilee
Why your joyous strains prolong
What the gladsome tidings be
Which inspire your heav'nly song

Refrain

Come to Bethlehem and see
Christ Whose birth the angels sing;
Come, adore on bended knee,
Christ the Lord, the newborn King.

Refrain

See Him in a manger laid,
Whom the choirs of angels praise;
Mary, Joseph, lend your aid,
While our hearts in love we raise.

O Come All Ye Faithful

O Come All Ye Faithful
Joyful and triumphant,
O come ye, O come ye to Bethlehem.
Come and behold Him,Born the King of Angels;
O come, let us adore Him,O come, let us adore Him,
O come, let us adore Him,Christ the Lord.

O Sing, choirs of angels,
Sing in exultation,
Sing all that hear in heaven God's holy word.
Give to our Father glory in the Highest;
O come, let us adore Him,O come, let us adore Him,
O come, let us adore Him,Christ the Lord.

All Hail! Lord, we greet Thee,
Born this happy morning,
O Jesus! for evermore be Thy name adored.
Word of the Father, now in flesh appearing;
O come, let us adore Him,O come, let us adore Him,
O come, let us adore Him,Christ the Lord.

Hark the Herald Angels Sing

Hark the herald angels sing
"Glory to the newborn King!
Peace on earth and mercy mild
God and sinners reconciled"
Joyful, all ye nations rise
Join the triumph of the skies
With the angelic host proclaim:
"Christ is born in Bethlehem"
Hark! The herald angels sing"Glory to the newborn King!"

Christ by highest heav'n adored
Christ the everlasting Lord!
Late in time behold Him come
Offspring of a Virgin's womb
Veiled in flesh the Godhead see
Hail the incarnate Deity
Pleased as man with man to dwell
Jesus, our Emmanuel
Hark! The herald angels sing"Glory to the newborn King!"

Hail the heav'n-born Prince of Peace!
Hail the Son of Righteousness!
Light and life to all He brings
Ris'n with healing in His wings
Mild He lays His glory by
Born that man no more may die
Born to raise the sons of earth
Born to give them second birth
Hark! The herald angels sing"Glory to the newborn King!"

26042911R00071

Made in the USA
Middletown, DE
17 November 2015